Northwest Vista C
Learning Resourc
3535 North Ellisc
San Antonio, Tex

"WHAT'S SO FUNNY?"

How to Get Humor and Good Storytelling into Your Speeches and Presentations

NORTHWEST VISTA COLLEGE

Whats So Funny How t

34009000185455

by Cherie Kerr

Illustrations by Sim Middleton

©Copyright 2000 by Cherie Kerr

All rights reserved. No part of this book may be reproduced or utilized in any form or by any means, electronic or mechanical, including photocopying, recording or by any information storage and retrieval system without permission in writing from the Publisher. Inquiries should be addressed to:

Permissions Department, ExecuProv, DePietro Performance Center, 809 N. Main Street, Santa Ana, CA 92701

ExecuProv Press

Printed in the United States of America

First Edition

ISBN#: 0-9648882-4-6

For
Nan-Heart
Laugh or cry, you're always there

ACKNOWLEDGMENTS

First and foremost, thanks to God for giving each of us an unlimited source—and sense—of humor.

Recognition to my parents, Margaret and Charlie—who raised my sister and me in a house where humor and laughter were not only encouraged—but a way of life.

Deepest thanks to my children (as well as my grandchildren—Cameron James, Brendan Stanford and Tianna Cherie)—you're what matters most.

Profound gratitude to those who help me in my efforts regularly to spread the gospel of humor to the business community: Shirley Prestia, Brian Spillane and Drake Doremus. And, a big "hats-off" to Drake: who's the funniest person I know!

Ongoing appreciation to the others who continue to applaud my work: Tom Maxwell, Dick Frattali, Michael Gellman, Tracy Newman, Julia Sweeney, and Gus Lee.

Affection to both the L.A. Groundlings and the Orange County Crazies who tickle my funny bone in its deepest part.

Enormous praise to those ExecuProv students who were willing to risk failure in order to prove to themselves they *were* funny, after all. Among them: Bob Crites, Bill Ellermeyer, Robert Thomas, Ed Poll, Ben Rasperry, Laverne David, Lowell Anderson,, Merry Neitlich, Mary Beth Whalen, Barbara Eilert, Sim Middleton, Gary Thermosgaard, Kristen Fenton, and Vicky Betancourt.

Indebtedness is truly an understatement when it comes to "The Girls." We will, no doubt, laugh together convulsively throughout eternity.

Deborah Way: thanks for the vicarious trip to Yale. Kendra Lee: You give new meaning to the term "support-system!"

Appreciation to Alex and Audrey for pushing me—and not letting up—each time I've needed it.

Much affection to Brenda and Rowena.

Don Cribb: You're such a gift to the arts and the world!

Judy: It's SBF forever!

Dad: Thanks for cracking me up from day-one. Mom: Wherever you are now—do you still laugh till you cry?

Heather, you soy-o…

"What's So Funny?"
Table of Contents

Introduction	Hey, You're Funny! (Everybody Is) 1
Chapter 1	A Funny Thing: Who Needs It? 9
Chapter 2	Now, That's Funny: Identifying .... 19 and Categorizing Humor
Chapter 3	Funny *You* Should Ask: Exploring Your .... 35 Own Sense of Humor
Chapter 4	The Funny Part About It: Five Things .... 45 That Make Humor Humorous
Chapter 5	Real Funny: Secrets of Delivering Humor 61
Chapter 6	A Funny Bit: The Almighty Icebreaker 77
Chapter 7	The Funniest Thing Is... : .... 89 What's Appropriate, What's Not
Chapter 8	Too Funny: A Time and a Place for Humor ... 105
Chapter 9	You Think That's Funny? How to .... 119 Create, Compose, and Gather Humor for Speeches and Presentations
Chapter 10	Not That Funny: Just Good Storytelling 135
Epilogue	Is *That* Funny? Sample Speeches— .... 149 Before-and-After Humor and Stories

Introduction

Hey, You're Funny! (Everybody Is)

Here's a reality: Most of us—no, strike that—*all* of us truly enjoy humorous speakers and presenters. We can't seem to get enough of them! In fact, we can't wait to get to that speech or presentation featuring the funny speaker. We'll even power-walk to the conference room just to get a good seat. What a treat: In the process of being educated or persuaded, we're also being entertained. We're actually having a good time. It almost feels like cheating, doesn't it?—having fun on the job!

The truth is, we business types need to have those who stand before us impart information in an entertaining way, preferably with humor. After all, we deal with enough dry material all day, every day. I know, for me, when it's my turn to attend a speech, I say: "Give me levity or give me a pillow," because if it isn't humorous or entertaining, then I'm taking a nap!

Some people call me crazy, but I firmly believe that everyone is funny. Funny in their own way, perhaps, but funny nonetheless. Some people are hysterically funny, while others possess a dry and sardonic sense of wit—they're straight-faced funny. Many others, of course, fall somewhere in between. And after years of my ExecuProv coaching and teaching business professionals how to improve their communications skills (I've been using improvisational comedy techniques to help people become better public speakers and one-on-one communicators for Fortune 500 companies), I believe that anyone who truly wants to explore and use their comedic gifts in a speech or presentation can—and will—comfortably and easily, once they learn how.

I've yet to know anyone—even to a small extent—whom I didn't find, at a minimum, amusing—or, the other end of the spectrum, hilarious. Our humor comes out when we dialogue with others—especially with the people with whom we're most at ease. During unguarded and spontaneous conversation, the best in each of us is usually brought forward. I'm talking about times when we go beyond the typical cordial banter—those other times when, without thinking, we throw out occasional quick-witted barbs; tongue-in-cheek remarks (that make those around us both laugh and identify); off-handed glib asides; and even longer, ear-grabbing moments, like when we share a fascinating personal story with someone we know.

One-on-one, humor seems like a snap for a good many of us, with the rare exception of people who are frightfully shy. Gabbing away in an elevator, chit-chatting on an airplane, or yakking away in an office lobby is no big deal. And to spontaneously say what we think, or how something makes us feel on the spur of the moment, is easier yet, and often very funny. But ask the majority of people to carry forth that same gift of quick-wit, great-gab, and take-you-there-storytelling in a speech or presentation and you might as well be asking them to bungee-jump off the Empire State Building. There's just something about trying a very conversational, off-handed delivery, rich with fun and humorous remarks, before an audience in a business setting—it freaks most people out. Sure, some business execs can muster enough courage to give a speech, but add humor? I don't think so! It's hard enough to pull off when you're in the midst of it, but planning it—oh, that's even worse.

For most of us, bantering around with *friends* is fine, but it's the speech or presentation in the *workplace* that does us in. The landscape shifts. Unlike the setting with your friends and family, there you are making your clever remarks and telling your humorous stories all alone. There's one of you, and a big, scary bunch of them. And they're all staring at you. Expectantly. Your sense of self-worth suddenly rests (heavily) on *their* reaction. The mere thought of planning out such a one-person show, complete with punchlines and pivotal, hard-hitting moments, evokes an unparalleled sense of fear. What if the "act" bombs? That fear alone can send you packing! If you're like most people, a certain sequence of thoughts start running through your mind. What if they just sit there? What if they don't laugh? Then what? Ah, the angst!

Many of my ExecuProv students say: "Making humor part of my speech is for the other guy. It's not for me. I'm just not funny." These students balk at the mere suggestion that they could liven up their speech or presentation with intermittent humor or storytelling. If I've seen it once, I've seen it a hundred times: when I broach the subject, their brow raises and their eyes suddenly bulge. Next, they freeze. After a few deafening seconds, they begin to stammer. Then comes the stutter. Finally they fall completely silent. Head down. Like a giant redwood, they petrify right there in front of me. "No," they softly plead, "I just want to give the speech, and that's all. I'll be happy if I can just get through the speech itself." When they say words to this effect, I ask: "Do you feel that way while engaged in conversation in the family room with your best friend?" "Huh?" is their knee-jerk response. I say it a different way: "Do you feel like you just want to get through it, to convey even the slightest bit of information or a story as quickly as you can when you're telling it to your friends and family?" They look at me like I'm nuts. I paraphrase again: "When you chat with friends and family, do you just impart facts?" "Oh...," they say, slightly defensive. "Well, no, but..." "No buts," I tell them.

The approach to sharing information with friends and family in the family room is no different than the approach to sharing information in the conference or banquet room. A room is a room, for goodness sake, whether you're in it chatting with friends and family, or educating some business-type on some *thing* or trying to persuade some business-type on some issue. Most people see the logic in that, but feelings don't have logic. Most of what we fear is what we feel.

If you're totally honest with yourself, you know you've delivered information to others with witty asides and humorous anecdotes; and you know that you did so with no trouble at all. Granted, it's probably been amongst those with whom you've been relaxed and comfortable. But nonetheless you did it.

After a moment of soul-searching, every one of my students who, at first, is certain they can't possibly "be funny" in their work-related speeches and presentations, eventually acquiesces. They (at times grudgingly) admit, "Okay, I've done it. I've said some funny things." "See, then," I tell them, "you *are* capable of communicating information in a humorous way; you just have to learn to transfer your humorous mindset from the family-room sofa to the meeting-room podium."

What truly saddens me is to know that most business folks are witty and clever and quick and charming at times when they didn't plan to be. You know how it goes: A zing here and a jab there, and once in a while a profoundly funny aside. And though I hate to say it, that kind of brilliant dialogue spews forth at times when it doesn't necessarily matter all that much. But rarely do these same people consider throwing out those same wonderful asides, adages, and great stories when delivering their speeches and presentations.

Often when I tell first-time students they can speak to an audience in a work-related atmosphere using those same gifts, they give me the old "Get out of here!." I've met cases. It's not because they don't want to be funny in a business setting, it's more a matter of thinking they really can't. But in the end, it's simply a matter of knowing *how* to do it—knowing how to transfer that same gift of humorous gab or storytelling into a speech or presentation. And that's the reason for the "What's So Funny?" class—and for this book. It's designed to take the guesswork out of the overall task. The *how* of getting humor and good storytelling out of you and into your speeches and presentations is the bottom-line goal of this book.

My ultimate wish is to convince each of you to actively and enthusiastically choose to integrate some measure of humor, comedy, or storytelling into each and every one of your speeches and presentations. Because, plain and simple: that's what your audience will always want.

Now, if you're one of those reading this introduction who has begun to closely assess and examine your ability to include humor and good storytelling in your speeches and presentations, and you're coming up with a resounding "No, I can't do it,"—if you're still convinced you're just *not* like the rest of the readers who have begun to realize perhaps they can be funny during speeches and presentations (as soon as they learn how)—then indulge me; go ahead and take the following simple quiz:

1. Do you sometimes have a funny thought when you're alone—a thought that makes you smile, or laugh out loud?
2. At times do you spontaneously blurt something out that elicits a laugh from the people around you?
3. Does anyone—your significant other, your children, or your friends—occasionally count on you to cheer them up when they are down? If your answer is "yes," think back to the most recent instance: was even a small measure of your verbal comforting expressed via some form of humor?
4. Has anyone ever said to you: "Hey (your name here), *that* was funny!"

If you answered "yes" to all four, you're going to have them rolling in the aisles and/or beaming broadly long after your microphone has been turned off. If you answered "yes" to three of them, you're home free! "Yes" to two of the above, means you, too, are a prime candidate for putting humor and/or good storytelling into every speech and presentation you ever make. In fact, you should never consider giving one without them. If you answered "yes" to only one question, don't despair: there's hope for you, too. If you answered "no" to all the questions, take the test again; I'm sure you missed something!

The lessons contained in the following chapters are meant to help you understand what constitutes humor and good storytelling; how to deliver information from a specific point of view; how to explore your own, highly personalized style and delivery of humor and storytelling; what's appropriate, what's not; when and where to use humor and storytelling;

and how to tell stories that are entertaining but not necessarily funny. The book will even teach you how to begin to write or outline your humor and stories.

At the conclusion, you'll take a look at a few speech snippets that started out "flat" and see how they translated to "one great show" as soon as they were peppered with humor and good storytelling. You'll also learn how a good many stand-up comedians sculpt their material and what it is they do to deliver it effectively. You'll also learn a few secrets and techniques of the improvisational comedy actor—ideas you can easily use to spice up your "acts" and be fast on your feet, especially when it comes to question and answer segments. Lastly, you'll be asked to play with all of these concepts and put them to work where it counts the most: in your own speeches and presentations. In the end, you'll have a terrific new point of view. You'll know "What's So Funny?" and why!

So enough of an introduction. Let's get started. Let's have some fun along the way!

"... so next thing I know it's stapled to my forehead!"

Chapter 1

A Funny Thing: Who Needs It?

If you're wondering why corporate America is often boring, just listen to the speakers and presenters who stand before you. Not all, but many of them drone on like sluggish washing machines—sloshing around a fact here and a figure there. And of course they run their tedious cycles on your time. You know that because you keep glancing at your watch.

I get antsy in a matter of minutes when I am made to sit still and listen to a boring speaker. The bad news is—at least in my experience as a business-community bystander—that the majority of speakers are boring, or, at a minimum, predictable. That's not to say there aren't great speakers out there now and again, but finding one in the workplace is rare. I often wonder: Why is it people think we're going to be fascinated with them when their material and their delivery is as flat as Kansas? Too many speakers assume their only task is to pass on information, or tick off the reasons why we should be persuaded to do something. They give us the info, sure. But where's the flair? Where's the color? Where's the surprise? Where's the punch?

Not long ago, I had a week when my business schedule called for attending several talks. During most of them I was in what I term "audience hell." Toward the end of this seemingly endless period, I began to lose patience. I had fantasies about doing lots of horrible things to the last speaker of the week—like duct-taping her mouth shut, for one. Somewhere in the midst of her statistical descriptions of different size Post-its, my mind drifted: I suddenly thought about getting a large net and quietly scooping her off the podium, then abruptly backhanding the prized catch right out the window. Instead of tomatoes, I considered throwing all 90 or so chairs toward the dais, just to liven up the place. "God, deliver me from those horrid slides," I prayed (the ones that listed a bullet point here and a bullet point there!). My attention span could take no more. Soon my mind checked out completely. Delirious now, I smiled faintly, recalling the time I'd stood up in the middle of a boring speech and loudly proclaimed that I thought the room was on fire: "Anyone smell smoke?" I'd blurted. That day I broke up both the crowd and the monotony. It was worth it, though, and I've never regretted it. I felt I was doing everyone a service, especially the speaker. I know I'm not alone in having had these experiences; everyone I know has had them, too.

AND THE TRUTH SHALL SET YOU FREE

The truth is, we all need to be entertained. I don't care if you're singing and dancing or you're speaking and presenting—a show is a show. There's an audience at either occasion. And what that audience not only wants, but *needs*, is to be kept interested, stimulated, and downright captivated. As speakers, it's our job to do that for people. But far too often, we tend to get the "stuff" all organized and stand up there and give them that. Maybe people need and want that "stuff", but not the way in which we dish it out. If we really want to get our message across—really want to make an impact—we need to tell stories and impart humor. If I were commissioned to author the "speaker commandments," this would rank at the very top: "Thou shalt not speak without humor or a good story."

AT OUR PARENTS' KNEES

If you recall, the first time you were spellbound listening to another person—getting involved as an audience member—was probably when you sat on mom or dad's lap or at their feet, listening to the stories they would tell or read to you. For most of us, that's how it all started! Sometimes these stories were happy, sometimes adventurous, sometimes suspenseful, sometimes sad, sometimes scary, and sometimes thought provoking (I still love *"The Little Engine That Could"*). But the stories I think each of us liked best were the ones that made us laugh. The funny ones. They always made us feel good. And I don't know about you, but when mom or dad told me a funny story (or read one to me), I always had that giddy sense of expectancy. I knew the fun was coming, and I couldn't wait. Sometimes the giggle would idle in my throat just waiting for the trigger that would release it. Nobody had to ask me to pay attention—I just did.

I'm not a kid anymore, by my joy in being entertained hasn't changed one bit. I don't think yours has, either. But how many speeches and presentations have you attended where the speaker sounded like he was just reading instructions off the back of a bicycle manual? So much for anticipation. Ho hum.

OUR EXPECTATIONS

For some reason, we've all come to expect—and accept, for the most part—the people who stand up before us will bore us to death. It's just the way it is; it's the corporate custom. The mindset is: Keep it serious. This is "business!" But lack of entertainment-value doesn't make the lesson or message easier to assimilate; rather, it makes it harder.

Those of us in corporate America have got to get business professionals to rebel and change! We've got to convince people that it's not only okay, but mandatory, to inject humor and good storytelling into every speech and presentation.

If you knew that each speech/presentation occasion would be full of laughs and stories, wouldn't you be looking forward to attending? I sure would! When was the last time people were fighting over chairs at your event for the chance to get a better seat? Anyone in your department scalping tickets this week to your sales pitch or training session? I don't care what level you're at as a speaker or presenter, you can give your audience a taste of your sense of humor, as well as a good story. It's your professional duty! It's what we all want and need from you.

HI HO, IT'S OFF TO KINDERGARTEN WE GO

Think back: When you packed up for kindergarten, did your hunger or need for a good story and a good laugh wane? No, not at all; in fact, you probably wanted more. And, in most classrooms during those early days, we got just that. Yippee—we got entertainment at school *and* at home!

Joyfully, we came to expect that's the way it would always be. If we sat quietly and well behaved, giving the person in front of us our full attention, we would be rewarded. That person would please us just like mom and dad, and our best babysitters, did. During those early days we sat at our desks, or cross-legged on the floor, waiting for something entertaining to happen. Something wonderful. Every lesson seemed to have a hook, a zing—something that thrilled us.

Well, I don't know about you, but shortly after kindergarten, as I began my ascent through the upward grades, I became sorely disappointed to learn that the people in front of the class—weren't making it as fun or interesting anymore. Little by little my happy face started to turn downward. Slowly but surely, the programming switched. Teachers—the people who used to make us smile and screech with glee—gradually made us squint and scowl. They transformed before our eyes. Bewildered, we sat by helpless, day by day, as we watched them become more and more austere. Their lessons became more serious. We weren't singing the alphabet anymore; instead, we were trying to find those letters and put them together in sentences. The teachers lost their touch *and* their grip on us.

Yet, although I was disappointed, I, like so many of my chums, just shrugged it off. Oh, well. We began to accept that this was the way it should be. For some of us, much later on, even our speech and debate instructors would emphasize the serious; even they would pay little homage to humor and good storytelling. It all seemed perfectly fine at the time: so grown up, so business-like. Soon, we would graduate and become just like them.

LETTING GO AND LETTING DOWN

So then, ever so slowly, many of us came to accept that the fun we once had in the audience was just not something we could count on anymore. Life not only became more serious, it also became more and more intense. Many of us learned through drills and rituals, not laughs and stories. "Save the fun for recess, or after school," Sister Carla, my fourth-grade teacher, a Dominican nun, admonished us. "Or when you're with mom and dad. *We're here to learn!*" Oh, so that's how it's done...

Ironically, though, many of us didn't learn as well or as easily as we had when we were being entertained in the process. I, for one, fall into that category. And because of that, every ExecuProv class I host is rich with fun; I truly believe my students will not only learn but retain much more! When standing before an audience, I always revert back to the way it used to be—to what I remember of how I was kept entertained and stimulated. I emulate that. I'm asking you to do the same. As you'll see in the upcoming chapters, it's actually easier to give speeches and presentations using humor and storytelling than it is to give it to them "straight".

MAKING THE HUMAN CONNECTION

Remember this: Your audience will always mirror you. If you're having a good time, so will they. How many speeches and presentations have you given lately where you were having a great time? If you can say all of them, I'm genuinely proud of you; if not, I want you to let go and reconsider your approach. I want you to imagine what it would be like to feel a real connection with that audience.

You may not have thought about it, but your job is to connect with every person in your audience. After all, we're all selling something—whether it's a product, a service, a philosophy, an idea, or, if you're an actor, a part. It's hard to sell if you're not connecting. And it's hard to connect if you're distant, stiff, rigid, and otherwise removed from the very people you're trying to get next to. I understand that getting "next to" and "with" an audience is something most people either don't know how to do or, often, don't enjoy. But if we're going to make speeches and presentations, it goes with the territory. It's part of our job. What better way to do it than through humor and good story telling!

I think if you were to consider going at your material and your delivery differently, you might discover a new comfort level in speaking and presenting to others. If you're one of those who does enjoy speaking, however, I'd still like to see you enhance and upgrade your "show" by doing the lessons in this book. They're designed to help everyone from the timid beginner to the outgoing showman. In the end, remember: Your job is to entertain. We all need to be entertained. We *want* to be entertained.

YOUR FAVORITE TEACHER

As you begin to evaluate the merits of injecting humor and good storytelling into your speeches and presentations, I want you to embark on your first assignment. I want you to go back in time and do a mental inventory of as many teachers as you can recall who were entertaining in some way. I feel safe in saying that each of us had at least one or two really "great" teachers when we were in school. These were the teachers who made us want to learn because as they stood up there in front of us each day, they put on a show! They were funny or passionate. Most often they were both. Because of their approach, we came to love the subject at hand.

For instance, I hated World History, but I had one teacher who went out of her way to make the subject interesting. I remember her giving us a behind-the-scenes look at the nature of Anthony and Cleopatra's relationship. She re-enacted a conversation between the two of them (using both feminine and masculine voices and stances, physically jumping back and forth, impersonating them both), illustrating how they fought over a strategy to save their prized territories. I was spellbound. Each day as I walked down the hall to this teacher's classroom, my mood became upbeat. My cadence was faster. I couldn't wait to take my seat. I had a constant sense of excitement. So did the rest of the class. We never knew what the hell Miss Davis was going to do. We loved it. She always had something humorous to say even if her mood was one of heavy drama on some days. She'd say things like: "I don't really think Cleopatra looked like Liz Taylor. Look at this photo, she had a nose like Jimmy Durante." There wasn't one day that she didn't throw out some quick-witted spontaneous remark or personal opinion that delighted us. We listened, we laughed, we learned. I never dozed off once during her class. (It was right after lunch, too—my nap time.) In fact, I often felt let down when the bell rang.

Next period was math. I dreaded it. Looking back, I realize now it wasn't so much math I hated (I love nothing more than to count my own money). The problem was the man who taught it. His voice was like a dial tone. His pitch never changed the whole 48 minutes, nor did his approach vary the whole semester. He was as predictable as a traffic signal; first, red, then yellow, then green, then red, then...thank God for daydreaming.

Take a few minutes and search your repository. You, too, probably had at least one teacher in elementary school, junior high, high school, or college who entertained the heck out of you! Who was it? Make a list of what made this speaker/presenter so wonderful. This is going to help as you proceed through the coming chapters

WHAT DO YOU WANT?

In addition to recalling that terrific teacher, who else in your life—past or present—falls into the category of being entertaining? We all experience speakers we like and dislike. It's time now to analyze those we like. As you go about making your list, I want you to include even stand-up comics who enlightened you in some way; either through new information or new insights about human nature. Notice how effectively they've imparted their message or sold their point via humor and stories.

HEY, YOGI—WHAT A PHILOSOPHER

I think it's safe to assume that most of us, given a choice, would much rather be fed information with humor and good storytelling. I know some speakers who get their messages across by just telling one story after another. That's such a clever way to inform or sell! It's almost impossible to tune out someone like that for even a few seconds.

Here's something else I want you to ponder: Most of us will forget 80 percent of what someone tells us during a speech 20 minutes after it's over. So it's the colorful bits—anecdotes, adages, famous sayings, pearls of wisdom, quick or witty "bytes"—that we easily call up months, and sometimes years, after a speaker has spoken.

I'll cite a reasonable example: Let's say you were in the audience listening to a speech by Yogi Berra—someone, incidentally, with a very dry wit and slow delivery (he's about as low key and straight faced as they come). Very funny in *his* own way (you'll find yours, too). To illustrate my point, let's put some words in his mouth; let's pretend he conveyed the following message to an audience in this way: "Ladies and gentlemen: I just want to say that most of you may think a situation has reached a conclusion when, perhaps, it has not at all. It's wise, then, to simply see a situation through to the very, very end before drawing any conclusions."

I'm sure you've guessed by now that this is a paraphrased (and very expositional version) of his very famous adage: "It ain't over till it's over." Now, Yogi said the same thing in both instances—in our made up example, and in real life. But it's the real-life quote that none of us will ever forget. The main reason it works is that it's humorous. None of the meaning or message is lost. In fact, it's even harder-hitting than the fabricated version—partly because it's shorter and more to the point, but mostly because it's humorous and brilliant at the same time.

If we could just begin to think about injecting a cleverly crafted or spontaneous remark of our own here and there, we would delight our audiences. If you don't feel inventive enough to create your own, you can always pepper your monologue with quotes from others (like Yogi)! Either way works, just so long as you do it! What's important is to think about how effective Yogi Berra has been by way of his famous "dugout philosophies." He's not only humorous (and he's not some great comedian, either!); he's memorable, and he's profound. Ask yourself this: If you were in the audience, which Yogi Berra version would you prefer hearing to take in the point he was trying to make? Now, consider what it is that people want from *you* when you speak and present. I think you know the answer: a funny thing. It's what we all need!

Chapter 2

NOW, THAT'S FUNNY: IDENTIFYING AND CATEGORIZING HUMOR

There are vast differences between the speaker who *tries to be* funny and the one who simply *is*. And, as you know, one of the primary missions of this book is to help you understand what those differences are—*why* they are. We need to get around to you and your sense of humor, yes—that's the main purpose of this book—but first let's look at other people; let's find out who is funny and why.

While subsequent chapters will address (and dissect) the mechanics of humor—the elements that constitute humor; how to incorporate these elements into your speech and presentation text; how to effectively deliver your material with humor in it; how to implement these new-found techniques in a practical and consistent way—this chapter will serve as a primer by considering those speakers and presenters whose sense of humor we admire and enjoy.

Some members of this group just may be folks in your work environs; however, I would bet most of them are not. Sadly, we find the majority of humorous people and good storytellers in the entertainment industry, usually among professional comedians. Most of these people, though you might never have thought of them as "presenters", are just that—they're just as much "public speakers" as we in the business community are. This chapter, then, will take a closer look at professional comedians; how their work is so closely related to ours and how we can capitalize on what they do so effectively. Don't forget what I tell all my ExecuProv students: a great actor is a great observer. I want you to go into observation mode. I want you to study the best. An intense look at some of the great comedic performers is a wonderful way to get in touch with what might work for you as you get your own humor ball rolling. Like my other students, you'll have come away with a deeper and more thorough understanding of the nature of humor and what makes audiences laugh. And the fun part is, I'm asking you to study who *you* like. You're going to find out why you laugh at your favorites. It wouldn't surprise me if you are one of those who, until now, has sat back and enjoyed your favorite brand of comedy without ever knowing why. It's one of those wonderful pleasures in life we all seem to take for granted, isn't it? But now, all that's changed! We're going to take humor apart and reassemble it, understanding what exactly makes it happen.

Think of this activity as though humor were a vacuum cleaner, for instance, or some other mechanical device. If someone showed you how to take it apart, piece by piece, and then put it back together again, you would begin to appreciate how one piece connects to the other. In the end, you would have a much better understanding of how and why the vacuum cleaner works. We're going to do the same thing with comedy. We're going to take it apart in order to understand it better. We're going to look at the whole idea of humor scientifically— to give you a better handle on using this tool in your speeches and presentations, to help you make your stuff work consistently, rather than occasionally. Because, as you can see, it's a little difficult to get right down to the *doing* of humor until you have a little better understanding of *what* it is and *why* it is, not to mention the particulars of *when* and *how* it affects you.

So for starters, I'd like you to do what I ask all my students to do: Get pencil and paper and make a list of what and, more importantly, *who* it is that amuses you, that makes you laugh. That's it—just make a list. And if you find yourself giggling or guffawing as you write—so much the better. No better way to do that than to study the masters. Think of it this way: If we were going to learn to make a great meal we might study the work of Julia Child (well, *you* might; but I, personally, would study the Stouffer family). Well, you get the idea. To learn about being funny, we're going to study people who are known for being funny. (Don't you wish we'd had a class like this in school?!).

HUMOR 101

Whether you've thought about it or not, there really are many different types and styles of humor. And, as we consider them, I want you to actually make this a serious study session—I want you to go to "comedy class."

Okay. Now that you're enrolled, think of this part of the book as "Humor 101." The objective at the end of the course is to identify what makes humor humor and what makes you and those around you laugh. As I tell all my students, there is not any better way to do this than to pull up a chair and a VCR, or your memory bank, and begin to study those who you see on stage and screen. Some may pleasantly amuse you, while others unexpectedly crack you up.

As you go about your assignments, don't panic: I'm not asking you to change careers, nor am I asking you to take to the stage and imitate any one comic. Moreover, I not asking you to deliver a speech or presentation in the mode of a stand-up comic or a sitcom actor. I only want you to get a better grasp of how the pros work. Because, after all, in theory, we're going to use a lot of what they use when they get up to perform.

SEEN ONE SEEN 'EM ALL

In the end, when it's all done and said, we're no different than the entertainers to whom I'm referring: We, too, are attempting to keep the interest and attention of our audiences. We're hoping to make them smile and laugh, make ourselves memorable and liked, win people over, and, of course, entice them into coming back for more. So in that respect, we're not any different from the stand-up comic or the sitcom actor: Our objective, like theirs, is to say something in an entertaining way. I firmly believe that it's not what you say, but *how* you say it. You can take the most boring material and really give it some kick.

Here's something to consider while you're studying the pros in search of the truth about humor: Be mindful that every comic has a mission, just like you. They, too, are trying to get a point across, sell their audience, persuade them, inform them. Just like you, they, too, are delivering some kind of message. So that's your first "interest in common" with the professional comedian. (Pay attention, now, because I'm going to give a quiz at the end of this chapter!)

As you go about the task of analyzing each pro on your list, see if you can determine what comedic choices they select to make their point—to get their message across. You can then begin to see how you can use some of their tricks—formats—styles—their ideas—to weave in and around your material as you share your message.

DIFFERENT STROKES FOR DIFFERENT JOKES

Some of us find particular styles of, and approaches to, humor funnier than others. I, myself, appreciate all types of humor—I find value in every kind. But I do have my favorites and I'm sure you do, too. I'm just as sure that you've never thought scientifically about how the various types of humor work. After all, putting humor under the microscope is not something you do each time a comic makes you laugh. You laugh, you move on. (Now, if you were an aspiring comic, you might intensely scrutinize *why* something was so funny. I know comedic actors who do that all the time! They're obsessed! But not necessarily the rest of us.)

So then, while some of us appreciate all types of humorous expression, I've learned over the years, that each of us is inclined to favor one over the others. To simplify our work, I'm going to suggest that we examine three basic types of humor: Physical, intellectual and emotional. It is from these three categories of humor that all others spring forth and take form. Yes, there are sub-categories, and the dissection of humor can become far more intricate and complex but for now, for our purposes we can confine ourselves to a big-picture view of what makes us laugh and how we can use these basic principles in our own work.

OH, THOSE WILD AND CRAZY GUYS

Physical comedy is our first area of study. We've all seen comedic actors who rely heavily on sight gags—physical actions or exaggerated facial expressions—to convey their humor. Prime examples of comics who have been, or are, stellar at physical humor include: Lucille Ball, Buster Keaton, Charlie Chaplin, Laurel and Hardy, and Jerry Lewis. More contemporary examples include Jim Carrey and the late John Belushi and Chris Farley. The early work of Chevy Chase (whose falls still make me laugh, especially the one of Gerald Ford deplaning the Presidential helicopter) and Steve Martin also provided a great deal of laughs from a physical vantage point. Martin had some gems—such as the slick walk of the "Wild and Crazy Guys" and those complex "Happy Feet" moves. For some, just the thought of the old slip-on-the-banana-peel is enough to bring on the laughs. Others love the pie in the face, the toilet paper on the shoe, the classic stomping of grapes (Lucille Ball in top form), the cold-cream on the end of a nose (Peter Sellers as Inspector Clouseau). Can you think of other examples of physical comedy? Again, I'm referring to those comics who use their bodies and their faces and often, props, in some form of activity or movement to say what they have to say comedically. As you make your list, don't forget those who never say a word. For example, the Keystone Cops, Harpo Marx, Ruth Buzzi as the old woman who knocked Arte Johnson off the park bench (*"Laugh In"*). Did you write down Rowen Atkinson (Mr. Bean)?

While this category may be the one you use the least to craft your style, you still may find value in using some interesting props or performing some physical activity as you stand before others. Examples: I once knew a judge who was trying to make a point about changing case law. As he took to the podium, he had his gavel hidden under his coat. Everyone thought his speech was going to be one more of those tedious and pedantic monologues—until he suddenly whipped out his gavel and began banging it on the lectern. He playfully threatened audience members with it, and once he even clobbered himself on the head—much to his audience's delight. With his physical comedy, he brought levity to what was otherwise a boring subject to most people. That audience perked up and sat expectantly throughout his 30-minute speech.

Another example of physical humor is the client of mine who told his audience about being late for a meeting. He was a printing salesman; the meeting was the first with a would-be client. As he talked about being late and the horror he felt at not being able to find the client's office, he began running in place, his eyes bulged, his breathing became shallow and rushed. He threw his head back as though he was running against the wind, his face contorted. His mere movements, re-enacting his fiasco, thrilled his audience. They couldn't help but laugh *and* like him.

Can you recall any speakers you know who used their "physicality" as a means to convey an idea humorously? Write them down alongside your list of comics who fit this category.

SOMETHING FROM NOTHING

Next, there are the comics who use intellectual humor as their communication vehicle—the reasoning and rationalizing types. Mort Sahl and George Carlin are two great examples of years past. Carlin's current material still blows me away. Later came Paul Reiser, Jerry Seinfeld, Dennis Miller, and Woody Allen. These types are constantly questioning, analyzing, probing, agonizing over, and diligently attempting to find reason and rhyme for human nature and the way of the world. They're the ones who are always trying to make sense of the senseless. If you study Woody Allen's work, for instance, you will find it is rich with philosophical query. Seinfeld, as we know, had one of the highest-rated sitcoms in history, presenting one "small" idea after another and analyzing the hell out of each. He covered everything, literally, from soup to nuts. Whether or not intellectual comics are your favorites, make a list of others who you think fit this category.

You have probably heard speakers who use intellectual humor, too. They're the ones we refer to as being "in their heads." Example: I once listened to a guy who was hawking a long list of office products designed for use by accounting firms. (This was years before computers). As he stood before the group, he began talking about the new eraser tip for a pencil. He showed it to the audience (they were all CPAs) and told them it wouldn't smudge and, unlike most pencil erasers, they wouldn't have to break it in. But suddenly he launched into a discourse on how he once smudged an answer to a math question during a test in third grade. He shared with us that he was anal, even back then, and tried to remove this smudge, resulting in yet another smudge. Now there was a hole in the paper, he said, and no place to put the math answer. "I have this thing about holes in paper," he confessed. "I still can't bear to use a three-hole punch and it was years before I could perforate a paper towel. My therapist told me to go ahead and eat just one piece of swiss cheese. He thought I might have a breakthrough."

We howled. He went on to say, "This is the only eraser that I haven't bitten the tip off of. Anyone else here do that?" He finished by digressing into a rhetorical discussion about third grade. "Why is it we only remember the trying times of third grade? I mean, does anyone even remember third grade?" He himself tried to: "What is third grade for? Why can't I remember recess or the teacher? Why is it I can only remember that damn smudge?" Pause, then: "Deep down, I wonder if that's why I went into office products. Is it some sort of need to recreate that experience? Make it right? Was third grade a defining grade for most of us?" Long pause, then: Anyway about this eraser..." He tried so hard to make sense of what wasn't sensible to him. His confessions endeared us to him. I don't even use pencils, and I found myself buying his brand on my next visit to Office Depot. His intellectual sense of humor made me think. This type of humor almost always does. That's what is so fun about it. And, I'm still probing the purpose of third grade!

Who else does "think" stuff? The range is broad. How about David Letterman's and Jay Leno's monologues? How about the work of Garry Shandling? His satire has me rolling. Don't forget to add characters to your list too, like George, from *Seinfeld*. He was always in his head.

THEY FEEL FOR 'YA

The next group—the third comedic approach we're covering—tends to stir us by tapping into our emotions, by getting us to feel or relate to something in their message. Though our eraser-guy skated on the edge of emotional humor (comedy always overlaps), I used it because the guy questioned something—third grade—and got us thinking about our own third grade experiences long after the accounting workshop was over.

When it comes to striking an emotional chord, there are many great comedians who approach their work this way. Bill Cosby comes to mind for me. I think he's one of the best storytellers there is—and not just on stage or through his recordings. I had the distinct pleasure of working with him during the 80s.

I was putting together a press conference for a tennis tournament Cosby was hosting. He entered a briefing room shortly before the event. I was alone with him for what was supposed to be a five-minute prep focusing on what he needed to know before stepping in front of the press in the next room. We sat down. He began to shoot the breeze and went into one story after another. I was mesmerized. We kept the media waiting nearly an hour as he toked on his cigar, leisurely leaning back in his chair, telling me some of his earlier experiences with the press. He talked about his fear, his uneasiness in those early days, and colorfully described exactly what he was going through trying to field questions. I could feel it with him! I could also relate. And, thinking back on it, I believe anyone who'd have been in the room with us would have also shared the same feelings.

While Cosby may not be your favorite, there are hundreds of others you may want to add to your list. Entertainers really seem to please us when they have a way of digging deep and sharing experiences that seem to resonate with our own reality—our fears and joys. How about Louie Anderson, for instance? He has a way of conveying his humor through the eyes of a child. Ever hear him talk about riding in the car with his father? He is forever making us feel things we'd long forgotten.

Richard Pryor is another comic who makes us feel. He has succeeded in this regard in many ways. During his early days, his acts contained material that spoke of rebelling against the establishment—the system. Many of us got caught up in his momentum and felt frustration with him. And talk about frustration: Many of us screamed alongside the late Sam Kinison, too. Tim Allen has made emotional statements about his "manhood" through his wonderful work—guys totally relate to the insecurity of not enough "machismo." Whoopi Goldberg has talked about career and motherhood, and, boy, when she talks about the perils of trying to "have it all," I stand up and cheer (laughing all the while, of course).What about the emotionally charged work of Bette Midler or Rosie O'Donnell? They, too, have a way of evoking very strong responses from their audiences.

I've mentioned only a few who fit the category of emotional comics. I'm sure as you go about your assignments in this chapter, you'll think of others. List those who you feel bare their souls! The ones who, as they do, hit you at a very core level.

A few more clues to help you with this list: Ever hear Joe Pesci kibitzing on a talk show? Richard Lewis sharing his darkest fears? Rodney Dangerfield begging for respect? There are a good many others who lead their comedy with their heart. Who are they?

I'll give you an example of one of my students—a story he told in class one day. The first time he told the story he simply gave us the facts, nothing more. The second time around, he told us the same story, but told it from the heart. His name is Bob Crites, and he heads Condor Freight Lines, one of the largest ground carriers in the country.

Bob's story was about a time he and his wife attended a convention. They drank pretty heavily, he confided, and when they returned to their hotel room after an exhausting day of activity, she crashed. He couldn't wake her. He needed to, though, because he had just bought a new pair of cowboy boots and couldn't remove them (as he spoke he tried to illustrate how tight the boots were—anyone who'd ever been in his shoes could empathize).

Bob's wife had agreed earlier to help him if he needed it. Knowing she was out cold, he began to panic as he tried to figure out how to remove the boots. He was, he told us, dumbfounded as he sat next to his snoring, lifeless wife.

Then he shared a hilarious, blow-by-blow description of what came next. Here's what he said: "I just looked down at Mary Jo and said 'This isn't funny, dammit, wake up. I'm in crisis here.' No response. I immediately went to the bathroom to get a drink of water. I threw cold water on my face, hoping that would help. I'd seen it in some old Gary Cooper movie. As I stared myself down in the mirror, I finally said in my best John Wayne, 'Now what, Pilgrim?' Angry, I kicked the cupboard door under the sink in utter frustration. It popped open. I had thoughts about calling my mother when suddenly I saw the pipe, the elbow pipe that carried the water from the sink to who knows where. I guess when the going gets tough, we all get resourceful. So I lay down on my back, put the heel of the boot inside the crook in the pipe—the elbow part—and began to scoot backward on my butt and elbows. I pried the boot loose. It worked. It actually came off. I thanked God repeatedly as I changed positions to work on the other foot. All in all, it took two hours, but I got my boots off. When my wife woke up in the morning, she remarked at how much she loved my new cowboy boots and how she couldn't wait to see me wear them to that day's festivities. She told me I looked just like a trucker. I just muttered something, I don't know…my eyes were bloodshot, and my back was sore. My ankles were also swollen, and I had a couple bruises, too. I was walking like I just got off a horse. I was pretty crabby and said something like 'nah, you wear them'. I put my slippers on. I didn't care what she or anyone else thought. For a second I thought about leaving my pajamas on, too, and maybe making some joke about being Hugh Hefner, but I was the president of the California Trucking Association at the time and didn't want to embarrass myself. But anyway, no more cowboy boots, I said to Mary Jo! She gave me a very strange look, but, frankly, I could have cared less. I was exhausted, and ooh, my ankles!"

What made this story so fun for all of us is that the second time around Bob "took us there." He let us re-live the event with him, physically, intellectually and emotionally. He told us what he was feeling, and we felt his sense of urgency and panic. We've all had a similar experience—getting stuck—and so it really hit home. We loved the uncertainty of how it would end, too. Pure entertainment. And very, very funny.

WHAT ABOUT THE OTHER GUYS?

We've just covered what I consider to be the three most important categories—or, approaches, if you will—to humorous expression. These are the three that I think will help you most as you go about finding your way to getting humor and good storytelling into your speeches and presentations. I do, however, want to take a moment to point out one other group of comics that might also be helpful to your study. They are not necessarily a category unto themselves, but they do have a particular style that I want you to become more aware of. I'm referring to the deadpan, or "straight man," approach to comedy. Sometimes people who use this approach make us laugh the hardest. In fact, their subtlety is magical. I, for one, love the understated in comedy. I'm sure you have one or two favorites, too. And, since your assignment in this chapter is all about what makes you laugh, I want you to give some consideration to deadpan comics as well.

Many in this category are my all-time favorites, by the way, such as George Burns, Jack Benny, Joey Bishop, and W.C. Fields. More current members of the genre include Roseanne, Gene Wilder, Chris Rock, John Lithgow, and Jane Curtin. Two of the greatest (and truly underrated comics of our time, I think) who fit in this milieu are Rita Rudner and Charles Grodin.

The late Phil Hartman was brilliant at any type of comedy, but I liked him best when he played the straight man—think of the 40s-has-been-wartime-film star on *Saturday Night Live* and the intense and prophetic character on NBC's *NewsRadio*. In a later chapter, we'll take a closer look at why this group's approach is so effective and how they convey their humor in this way. I do want to mention that impeccable timing is the single most important element in their comedic success—not their material and "natural ability," as some might argue.

Okay. Once again, it's time to make another list. I just gave you some of my favorites. It's your turn now to scribble down your "deadpan" choices. Including them in your study will be extremely helpful in laying more foundation on which to build your humor.

HIDDEN MEANINGS

Before we move on to having you explore your very own gift for humor, I want to make sense of what we've done so far and why it is I asked you to study the first three comedic categories. In each case—with every comic I used as an example, as well as real-life examples of those who I've seen give speeches—what made them so successful was this: Every one of them did the same thing; they shared with us their *innermost thoughts and feelings*. If you're looking for a major key to understanding what makes an ordinary story or an ordinary message funny or interesting, learn the following from the pros: they almost always take us there, take us inside their heads and hearts, and share with us what they were thinking and feeling at the time. (Even if the time is the present. Example: I once heard a student of mine say at the beginning of her speech: "I'm really scared to be up in front of all of you doing this. Is there anyone out there who would like to take my place? Big pause. "I'll give you my car!") Remember what amuses us is not so much about what happened; it is what someone is experiencing, what they are thinking; what they are feeling at the time. The magic comes in the communication of the feelings and thoughts involved with the experience. Much more on this later.

For now, here's what I want to do to sum up your lessons from this chapter:

1. Make a list of what you learned from studying the professional comedians you enjoy—those who make *you* laugh. Did you come upon some revelation you hadn't considered before? Example: Joe Pesci makes me realize how neurotic my whole Italian family is. I can share this in my speechmaking as I rationalize why I do certain things." How about you? Anything new about you or those around you that you hadn't realized before?

2. Make a list of your favorite comedians according to the categories we covered: Physical, Intellectual, and Emotional. (Deadpans, too.) Try to add a small note next to each one identifying a specific performance they gave that you liked. Example: Next to Garry Shandling, I wrote *The Larry Sanders Show*. Keeping these notes will be helpful later on. They can serve as great reference material. They will also be good for further study and for inspiration along your speechmaking way!

3. Make a list of what makes you smile and what makes you laugh. For instance, I crack up when Eddie Murphy talks about his father coming home from his job at a toy company, and how all they had to eat were toys. He goes on to describe his father doling them out, and his siblings fighting over them—are you laughing? I sure am. Soon you'll find funny things that just hit you harder than others. There are themes in all of us. They come from our experiences, our fears, our joys…You'll see why this is so important later on. Make record of your findings. This is a great basis for building your own comedy repertoire.

4. Watch the people around you as they laugh. Remember: A great actor is a great observer. For instance, when I'm writing sketch comedy (always satirical in nature), I tend to observe everything from a sketch-writing mode. I'm also more aware of what people find amusing about current events. Not only do you want to discover what makes you laugh; take a few moments to gauge the responses of others. This, too, will have meaning later on.

5. Take down a few notes on what you know you have in common with professional comedians. They, too, are trying to make a "sale" (an idea, a point, a piece of logic, a rationale). In that respect, they are just like you and me. They, too, are sometimes self-conscious in front of others. Also, they desire approval and positive responses. Can you think of other areas in common? Good. Write them down.

In closing, I want you to realize that it is through sharing the truth—telling others what you think and feel—that you will make people laugh. It's what the pros do—which is precisely why I'm having you study them: *They tell us the truth!* Honesty is as fundamental to humor as H^2O is to water.

I want you to strive to share the truth and study it in those you deem to be funny. It's a big key to making humor work. Whenever anything is contrived, we tend to know it. Even if the truth is exaggerated (Richard Lewis is a good example), the humor has still emanated from a genuine place. So think a lot about sharing the truth; I promise, it will always get you laughs and legitimize humor in any speech or presentation.

One more quick example: I remember an art director giving a presentation—what they call an agency review—to a group of automotive corporate executives. He had his display on an easel. The easel kept falling over. He kept right on talking, though (these reviews are often on a time clock), but on his way down to assume an Indian-style seated position on the floor, he finally shoved the easel aside and quipped, "I have this horrible feeling you guys are going to hold this against me and, hey, I worked on this all night…but I'm begging you…" he paused to think "oh…, maybe I should just finish this on my knees…" The room cracked up. So again, think a lot about the truth; it lays at the heart of workable humor. Most of us have "been" where others have been, and it is in the "going there" that we tend to have such fun! Yes, think a lot about the truth—it will guide you as you troop successfully along your humor and storytelling path.

Now that you have a clearer picture of what makes you laugh, it's time to move forward and begin to explore and pull from you your own innate talents as an entertaining performer.

We're one step closer now to helping you make your presentations and speeches more humorous and interesting!

Chapter 3

FUNNY *YOU* SHOULD ASK: EXPLORING YOUR OWN SENSE OF HUMOR

Now that you're beginning to understand what makes you and others laugh—and most importantly, why—it's time to explore your own innate ability to be funny (and to be a good storyteller) and what you can do to make people laugh. We all have it in us to be humorous. The challenge (it's two-fold) is: identifying your own particular style, so you can capitalize on and develop it; and learning various ways to bring forth your gifts when you need them the most—when you're delivering a speech or making a presentation. This chapter is all about discovering and exploring your very own personal brand of humor. Later we'll talk about how to put it to use in those critical, stand-and-deliver moments.

WHAT'S YOUR THING?

It's time to identify what type your sense of humor is. Your work assignments in the previous chapter were the first step in helping guide you toward that determination. You analyzed what you liked in others—mostly the pros—but now it's time to study *you*. Into what category do you think you fall? Are you more intellectual? More emotional? Just plain funny with your facial expressions or your physicality? What about brilliantly witty in a low-key or straight-faced way? It may be that your sense of humor overlaps and that you have more than one way of conveying it. But for now, I want you to zero in on what you think your dominant "thing" is, because it's the next step in getting you closer to our goal—beginning to use your humorous side to liven up your speeches and presentations.

YOU'VE GOT A FRIEND

One helpful way to zero in on your brand of humor is to ask friends and family members to give you some feedback. Ask someone close to you to recollect times when they thought you were very, or even slightly, funny. Maybe it was during a moment of minor crisis (you were physically comical while trying to regain your composure after falling on your butt on the tennis court). Maybe it was the time you shared a fearful or embarrassing story (my best friend told me about the time she accidentally kissed the pediatrician's hand rather than her daughter's, while bending down to comfort her daughter when she was being stitched up). Maybe something as simple as participating in conversation with others (times when you were witty and "on" with friends or business associates).

Make a list of your closest and most reliable (honest) friends and family, and give them a call. Ask them: "What's the funniest thing you think I ever said or did?" I'm willing to bet that each of them will come up with at least one humorous memory. Possibly more. Even if they have to think about it for a day or two, insist that they get back to you.

If you're not sure into which category you fall—where your comedic style lies—this research will serve as a great tip-off. After calling enough friends and family, you may begin to see a trend—a theme in your brand of humor. Maybe it will become apparent that you're the funniest when you're openly rationalizing something (intellectual humor). But whatever your friends and family tell you, pay attention to what they have to say.

DEAR DIARY

I'm guessing that you haven't kept a journal of all the times at work, or in your after-office life, when you were funny. I don't suppose you recorded those moments for some type of memoir. So your next assignment is to take a quiet time-out—preferably a whole afternoon or evening—and go back in time (as far back as you can recall), making notes of those instances when you just *knew* you were funny.

We've all had those experiences. For example, I was sitting in a class one day when someone said something about the world being full of difficult people—only they used a stronger word than "difficult." The guy said, "The world is full of... (it was a two-syllable word referring to a part of the human anatomy)." I quickly chimed in with, "I know. I married all of them." Then I went off on a tangent about my three marriages and my subsequent marriage-phobia.

Through sharing similar experiences that dealt with my feelings—emotional humor—I realized that that brand of humor was truly my strong suit. Taking that realization one step further: As I began to write sketch comedy, I discovered that satirical pieces—wherein I divulged my anger, my fear, my secret desires, my insecurities—or where the emphasis was on my emotional triggers and responses—seemed to get the biggest bang—rave reviews from both audiences and critics. I know now that the type of humor that suits me best has to do with an emotional release of some kind. Emotional humor is my primary "brand"—my "thing." What's yours?

TRUE CONFESSIONS

Once you begin to write down instances when you were genuinely funny, and gather feedback from those who know you best, you too will begin to see a pattern emerge. This will guide you in identifying your comedic/storytelling strength. And finding that strength at the outset is a crucial key to moving you toward developing your style and subsequently the material you choose for your speeches and presentations.

This may take some time, but what I suggest is that you sit quietly and recall certain "passages" in your life in order to recall your humorous moments. Do you remember a funny story your parents tell about you when you were a pre-kindergartner, for instance? How about some of those clever teenage pranks you played on your best friend?

I was told very often about the time my parents were dressed and ready to play their evening cocktail-lounge gig when suddenly they became captivated by the impersonations I started doing—impersonations of everyone in the family. I was four. My parents were so responsive to my burst of humor and my "coming out" (I had always been very shy up to that point) that they called musician friends to replace them at work so they could continue to watch my three-hour stand-up comedy routine. In truth, this must have been the beginning of my wanting to be a comedian.

I had periods in my life when I was hysterically funny; other times when I was trying to be cool, I was more subdued. But throughout different "passages" in my life, I was at my comedic best. And I know you were, too.

TRACKING YOURSELF

If you're not sure if you're on the right track, I'll give you a great clue to recalling your humorous highlights. Think back to times when you were spontaneous and went off on a discourse (like the one I just mentioned about myself)—opining or blurting out funny things you didn't even know you were capable of saying. Times when you were feeling perfectly free and open. We've all had spontaneous moments. (In fact, we could all use a lot more of them!)

But what if your memory fails you? You can still do this exercise by starting from scratch. Ask friends and family. Better yet, keep a journal for a month or so and write down all those moments when someone laughs (in a positive way) at something you do or say. Again, you'll begin to identify your "brand" in just a short time. And even if keeping a journal seems like an odd thing to do, remember: it's all part of your search-and-recovery exploration.

I'm adamant that you commit wholeheartedly to this identification process because I believe, as a result of working with hundreds of ExecuProv students, that it is only when we realize what comes most easily to us that we come upon our humor and storytelling brilliance. After coming upon it, we can capitalize on it. And the good news is this: Things that seem to come naturally to us take little effort. When you inject your own personal magic into your speeches and presentations you're going to find that it isn't nearly as tough as you thought it would be. You may also find that using your gifts is just plain fun. We tend to have a good time with things that we do easily. So dig for your own brand of humor if you have to; it's essential.

WORK IT OUT

Maybe your humor muscle is a little flabby. But with enough exercise, you'll tone it up and make it stronger. The idea is to pinpoint your brand, then put it to use. Before long, it will become something that you lean on in speeches and presentations especially during those oft-tense question-and-answer periods.

So once again, your homework is to recollect times when people genuinely laughed at things you did or said. You need only a handful, but if you simply can't remember even a single time, your job is to track those moments on a daily basis when you grace people with your humor in a small or big way. The object is to write it all down.

It won't be long before you say to yourself "Of course, I'm funny when I…" or, "When I do *that*, I'm really interesting and captivating." Soon you'll be far more conscious of your under-utilized talent for entertaining others and for getting the responses you want. Smiles and laughter are what you're after when others expect you to be dull and boring. If you haven't been thoroughly entertaining so far, your audience is in for a surprise!

Let me congratulate you now for doing this part of the self-examination. You're on your way to understanding what will make you a hit.

YOUR FIRST EXPERIMENT

Now that you've labeled *your* brand of humor, it's time to start playing with it. Here, then, is another assignment. I want you to take a low-risk situation, preferably at work, and respond to people, or share information, using your humor muscle. For instance, can you communicate information in a memo in a more colorful way—with a tad of humor, perhaps? Can you report back to your subordinates the goings-on of a meeting, providing a description of all the details with a little punch? Don't forget: The idea is to channel your humor and storytelling by way of your brand. Give it your personal humorous touch. As you do this assignment, keep the information you relay and impart as spontaneous as possible.

Here's an example: the before and after of a memo. It's a real-life example as provided by a client of mine—who turned in his homework to me for grading!

Take One: <u>The Memo</u>

Enclosed are the six copies of the publications you requested for duplication. As I understand it, the by-lined articles in them will be used for photostats, and those will be photocopied in large quantities for my press kit.

Kindly take very good care of them as they are my only copies.

David

Take Two: <u>The Memo</u>

Enclosed are the six copies of the publications you requested for duplication. As I understand it, the by-lined articles in them (and don't forget my picture), will be used for photostats (whatever those are), and those will be photocopied in large quantities for my press kit (and sent to everyone in the media, I hope!).

These are my only copies, so if you lose them, there will be execution by firing squad.

David

Correct me if I'm wrong, but I am far more entertained by "Take Two," yet I still get the same message. The way it's written makes me want to read and continue reading, because I like the tone immediately, and I'm delighted by the anticipation of what might come next.

Another example: I used to work at an advertising agency, and we had one account executive who put humor in every memo. We couldn't wait to receive them. People would literally line up and read over the shoulder of the person who pulled one of this guy's memos from the inter-office envelope (those used to be very vogue). My favorite one came about when Lyn (the AE) was asked to write the obituary column for a civic newsletter that the ad agency produced on a monthly basis. The president of the agency wanted something different. Well, Lyn sent around a memo asking people what they thought of his new approach. It read: "Hey, guys, tell me what you think. 'Dead, that's what Jim Brown was today'..." We could always count on Lyn to bring levity to the weirdest situations.

Maybe the two "takes" are not your style, but that's okay. And, really that's the point. What *is* your style? Write a few memos or notes of your own, the kind that you might circulate to people around the office—and see if you can craft them with some fun. (These have to be "low-risk" situations, remember.) This exercise will stimulate your creativity, prevail upon your sense of spontaneity, and begin to get you into the spirit and habit of using your humor brand (and muscle) on a regular basis. I firmly believe that if you tone your humor muscle, it will be ready to go into action in knee-jerk fashion anytime, anywhere—whether your find yourself having to write a last-minute speech or fielding an audience's unexpected questions.

PUT YOUR MOUTH WHERE YOUR PEN WAS

Now that you've mastered a little humor and good storytelling in your memos, it's time to try to the same thing in conversation. I'm not going to ask much of you. I'm simply going to ask that you try once a day to infuse a little humor in your presentation of something. For example, let's say you have to explain the new computer system that is going to be installed in the offices next week. Let's say there's a meeting, and you have to say a few words to those in attendance. Rather than provide them with just the facts, why not slip a little humor in there?

Here's a pretend scenario of what might typically take place in that situation: "Well, everyone, just wanted you to know that next week we'll be converting our current Microsoft system into the latest version of Word. It may seem a bit disruptive, but our department is asking for your patience until all is said and done. And, please, don't call us unless it's really necessary."

Now, that's nice. This quick presentation of information to the group gets the job done, yes, but is it interesting or fun? I don't think so. Instead, let's try this approach: "Well, everyone, just wanted you to know that next week is hell week. We'll be converting our current Microsoft system into the latest version of Word. In fact," (pause) "Bill Gates will be here in person to help us. Just kidding! I wish! So bear with us through all the disruptions, and if it really gets to you, well," (Long pause) "don't call us—call your mother, because we'll be" (Short pause) "calling ours!"

Same information, but delivered with a little levity. By the way, I don't think this second "take" would offend anyone in the room. It would instead, I believe, provide a little relief for a short time given the computer-hell ahead. Also, it establishes great rapport—the single most important element to connecting with people. Besides, people tend to appreciate your being direct and real. I know if I had to go through "hell week" and it started getting to me, I'd have a smile on my face just thinking about calling my mother to whine about it (even though my mother happens to be in the big office in the sky).

People tend to remember the fun things we say. So that's your next assignment. Take at least one situation where you have to inform or persuade a group (two or more people), and see if you can offer a little levity in the message. This, too, is one more wonderful way to practice exploring your overall sense of humor.

REMINDERS

Don't forget: Both these situations—the memo-writing and the mini-speech—must be practiced in low-risk climates at first. Later you can up the ante by trying such personal adventures in higher-risk situations such as a speech or presentation. (I think we all feel terribly at high risk during these times!) For now, the idea is to get you into the swing of it all. By that I mean doing the "brand" test and toning up your humor muscle by working it out.

EVERYTHING MUST CHANGE

If you do the above assignments—write a memo with a touch of fun and deliver some information with a little flair—you will begin to see how your humor muscle gets strengthened. You'll note that, for one thing, you're now beginning to prepare your thoughts and material differently. You're also beginning to rely a little more on the right side of your brain—(the more creative, spontaneous, and playful side), as opposed to always leaning on the left side (the reasoning and practical part of your thinking mechanism). (Yawn.) Too, both these assignments provide you with an opportunity to practice until you feel comfortable enough to play the humor/good storytelling game in a bigger arena. This part of your training is meant to condition you, yes, but what I think is more important is that it allows you to discover and become at ease with your own unique persona in an exciting and rewarding way. You'll learn things about yourself you may not have noticed or appreciated before.

Now that you've gotten a handle on understanding your brand of humor and experimenting with it, it's time to delve into some of the basic mechanics of what makes humor, humorous! In the next chapter, we'll lay some groundwork from which to launch that particular humor brand of yours.

Chapter 4

THE FUNNY PART ABOUT IT: FIVE THINGS THAT MAKE HUMOR, HUMOROUS

Some say that being funny or entertaining is an art. I won't dispute that; I agree. But along with the art, there comes a certain amount of science, too. If you doubt this, just consider that there are literally hundreds of comedy schools springing up all over the country—schools whose mission is to teach people who aspire to become successful in this art form exactly what it takes to do so.

Some institutions offer classes in scene study that exclusively address written comedic material (Neil Simon plays, for example). Other organizations and institutions focus on the study of comedic performance techniques such as those used in improvisational comedy or stand-up comedy. Though different schools concentrate on different aspects of comedy, they all cater to would-be actors who want what you want: to deliver content in a humorous way. Like you, these would-be actors simply need to discover how to draw comedy out of themselves—and how, scientifically, it's done. In other words, they take great care in learning the mechanics, just like you're about to do.

So, if you're one of those who believe you either have it or you don't, do not despair—as I mentioned earlier, we all have "it" in some form; we just need to understand it better and extrapolate it from our own unique talent pool. Breaking down good storytelling and humor is a great first step, especially for you skeptics.

In this book, it is primarily the tools of the stand-up comic that you'll study the most. By focusing on some of the basics of what they learn, I'm going to help you get off the ground in a humorous and good-storytelling way. Of course, since my specialty is improvisational comedy, I will also throw in some improv tricks and secrets, rules and tools—to help you understand the more clinical side of constructing and delivering your stuff.

In this chapter, you'll learn what many stand-up comedy performers and improv actors are taught. For, after all, they spend hours analyzing and dissecting the "why" and "what" of humor. Often, they do this through a series of rigorous exercises and drills. But first, like you, they must learn the basics, so that in the end they have the know-how to deliver their material in a most effective and successful way—whether their material consists of one-liners, sight gags, sketches or just downright entertaining stories.

What in the world is it that comedians learn? Keen insight and proven technique—both of which ensure that they will have a consistent performance each and every time they get before their audiences. And, getting your hands on their secrets is what we're up to now!

TAKE TWO PARTS OF THIS, ADD TWO PARTS OF THAT...

Though there are many ways to undertake the study of comedy, I have distilled, over the years, a formula that I've proven. It isn't necessarily a revolutionary forumula, but is original in that it combines certain elements I've mixed and matched to finally arrive at what I think works for my students—not just occasionally, but every time, in every speech or presentation. If followed systematically, the formula works in terms of successful delivery, whether your goal is to put across humor or just a good story.

So then, this formula is comprised of five basic components, each of equal importance. They are: energy, spontaneity, self-expression, timing and attitude.

I want to stress from the get-go that if any one of these five basics is missing, your "act" runs the risk of bombing. But if you stay true to every aspect of the formula it will be impossible for you to fail, no matter who you are or what your current level of expertise!

WE INTERRUPT THIS FORMULA TO BRING YOU THIS IMPORTANT MESSAGE

Prior to breaking down the formula to help you understand its five crucial elements, I want to say a bit about stage presence, because without the ability to "fill the stage with your presence," you will not command the attention and respect of your audiences. Haven't you seen speakers who practically whisper (even though they have the benefit of a microphone)? Speakers who mumble and slur their phrases? Who warm up their voices on your time?

Perhaps you already have wonderful skills in this area, but even so, let's review them. For those of you who don't, consider this a crash course.

There are three essential things you need to possess in order to be professional "on stage": breathing, diction and good vocal production (sound).

Proper breathing technique—breathing from the diaphragm in order to stay comfortable, and provide the necessary strength (or "air-push"), to project your voice and capitalize on its resonance—is at the core of *everything* in terms of what it takes to be a good performer. Without good breath control your voice may shake. It might sound tinny, or even monotone (God help us all!), and it may get hoarse or tired, too. If you breathe properly, none of the above should occur. But if any of the above sound familiar to you, you may need to get hold of some breathing exercises—deep breathing—so that when you speak, you sound more seasoned.

Something else about proper breathing: Because it affects your phrasing, it allows you to have great control over your timing (a major key to your humor or storytelling successes). So start working on building up the strength and power in your diaphragm. Don't rely on your breath coming from the top of your lungs; that's when you hyperventilate! Also, if you're one of those who gets the jitters, or even panics, proper breathing is essential because it stabilizes you.

The next area to spend a few moments on—and I'm militant about this one (just ask my students)—is good diction. All of us really dislike performers—speakers or comics—whose words are unintelligible—who run their words together—whose words we have to strain to understand. Often, they let the ends of their words trail off, or they sound muddled, which leaves us frustrated and antsy because we're trying to decipher their message. (I almost lunged for the dais once and shook the hell out of a CEO for this!) Take note: If your diction is poor (and I think this is epidemic in North America), people will lose instant respect for you, and that's the last thing you want. Luckily, there are ways to get this particular stage skill in good form. For one: practice tongue twisters. They're terrific. It doesn't matter if you can recite them perfectly; what matters is that you're working out your mouth—both jaws and tongue. You can also talk with a pencil between your teeth—my favorite—for a few minutes a day (all my students have to do this). Place the pencil between your upper and lower teeth—in the front, where it's harder to grasp—and begin speaking. Once you remove the pencil, you will quickly notice how easy it is to move your mouth around your words. Also, you'll finish each word rather than having the ends of them trail off. People will be able to understand everything you say! They'll fall in love with you! Good diction is essential to executing your comedic or storytelling material. Think about all the comics you like: almost all have great diction.

Finally, you want to foster good vocal production. Vocal production is basically the sound of your voice; how you use it depends largely on how you train and nurture it. That means you need to warm up your voice so the sound is full, rich, and complete. You want to use all the wonderful nodes in your voice box, not just a few. Some speakers pull on certain vocal chords (repeatedly) and get an irritating sound (usually a higher pitch than what is normal for their "sound"), and it's grating! So you must warm up your voice and train it to be fully used. By the way, if you breathe properly, you will push air past all those nodes, which gives you a head start on a fuller sound. Without vocal warm-up, though, you can't get a consistent sound.

Great actors always use their voices to the max, because their voices are what puts them across so effectively. They are religious about vocal warm-ups and work-outs. They spend ample time warming up and stretching their voices before every performance, thus expanding and utilizing all their vocal capability.

Here are a few tricks for better vocal production: Before your next performance, speak out loud, sing the musical scales, or recite a little Shakespeare. All of these will force you to use more of your voice. They will also wake it up! Anything else you can do that necessitates the use of your voice without hurting it (no screaming!) will work. In other words, do anything that generates noise. As I tell all my actors and ExecuProv students, you have mostly your face and voice with which to communicate, so make good use of them.

If you are already familiar with these fundamentals of stage presence, make sure you spend enough time working on them every day. Even veteran stage actors do this, no matter how many years they've been performing. There is nothing worse than enduring a non-professional speaker. You don't want to be a speaker gasping for breath; those are the types that freak out with fear-of-speaking-phobias—the ones you want to call the paramedics for. Nor do you want to be a speaker who runs words together—speaking with only the lower jaw in motion (and not much motion, I might add; don't they look like ventriloquist dummies?). You want to move both jaws—the entire mouth—to phonate—to get the sound out. And you don't want to sound like your voice is still asleep; those speakers' voices sound raspy, tired, thin… Even on a subconscious level, your audience will get irritated because you're warming up on their time. You know how it is: After a minute or two you're tuned up ready to go. Wrong! You need to start out strong and end stronger.

So stage presence is a must! I'm counting on you to get these essentials in order. They will set you apart from the amateurs. They will also provide a great foundation as you make your way toward adding humor and good storytelling to your speeches and presentations. If you practice regularly, you won't have to think consciously about them; they will become as automatic as the responses you use while driving a car.

YOU CAN'T HAVE ONE WITHOUT THE OTHERS

Now, back to the formula. Once again, the five elements for an effective delivery and for making humor work are: energy, spontaneity, self-expression, timing, and attitude. If any of these is missing, chances are your material will fall flat. If you include all of them in any speech or presentation, you'll always hit a home run.

Our first task is to break each element down to understand it better. Next, you'll practice individual drills that focus on each element in order to build up your strength and skill. After getting a handle on each element, then you can blend them together and use them in every speech and presentation to ensure you're reaching your humor or good-storytelling goals. Think of these elements—used in combination—as the foundation to buttress every humorous moment and every good story. It's the recipe for dead-on delivery!

FIRE UP

Let's start with the slab on which to build everything: energy. Without strong energy burning beneath your delivery, you can't put across the needed punch when telling a story or a joke. Energy is what everything rides on. It's hard to get any momentum—and humor especially relies on momentum—if you have a low energy level. So, you need to fire up. This doesn't mean you have to be hyper, by any means; many great comics have a more introverted energy display. But even those comics need to get a spark going before they take to the stage.

Actually, I think most of us fall into one of two categories: We're either more introverted with our energy, or extroverted! Charles Grodin and Kelsey Grammer are examples of the former, while Martin Short and Robin Williams represent the latter. People like Steve Martin, Billy Crystal, and Whoopi Goldberg fall somewhere in between. The point is this: Everyone who performs does so using energy as the fuel that supports their delivery. You can't expect to get up before others and make a humorous point or tell a great story if you have a sense of inertia. It's like trying to ski with no speed, or trying to barbecue with no flame.

There are many ways in which to promote strong energy before any speech or presentation. You can sit and rub your hands together; feeling the heat puts you directly in touch with your inner energy (you *are* energy!). You can talk loudly non-stop for several minutes (complaining about things that really bug you). You can run mental laps in your mind (run a laundry list of all the things you have to do for the day). Or you can physically pace. It doesn't matter what you do to get a little fired up, but you must get physically and mentally stimulated in order to have the momentum you need to secure a strong delivery.

I know you've seen speakers who are trying to deliver a great joke or a story but because their demeanor is sluggish or drab, it just doesn't execute. There is no room for "lackluster" when it comes to convincing your audience you're funny or captivating. Energy alone can put any material across (good and sometimes not so good). Remember that energy equals momentum, a must-have during any performance.

DOING WHAT COMES NATURALLY

The next element in our five-part series is spontaneity. If you force your joke or story, it will flop. I always tell my students to think first about the "beat points"—the pivotal and essential connecting points of a story. Then, as you go from one point to the next, you simply fill in the in-between parts spontaneously. It's easy to do. Let's say you know the punchline or the point of your story or humorous aside before you deliver the information; in that case you just use the beat points as guideposts. Don't worry about getting all the details that build up to your humorous materials or stories exact. You don't want each word to be perfectly scripted (canned); instead, just keep it as improvisational as possible.

When you're improvising your precious story tidbits along the way, you remain spontaneous. It is through the fluid state of spontaneity that we delight our audiences—and often, ourselves!

I challenge my students with this: Don't ever deliver the same story the same way twice. Do something different each time. If you're sharing a funny incident that happened to you, see if you can add or change a little something each time. For instance, though the punch line (the outcome) is always the same, see if you can tell the story from several points of view. Tell it once from the perspective of what you were thinking and feeling at the time it occurred; next, tell it from the vantage point of those who were involved in the situation with you; and next tell it from the bystander's vantage point. Anything that will add a little variety will always keep your stories fresh and new. So trust yourself and wing it a little when you inject humor or a story here and there in your speeches and presentations. Again, remember the overall point (or the ending)—but dance with it!

I'm sure you have seen speakers who have clearly told the same old, stale joke a hundred times. The tip-off: The audience's laughter is rather slow and delayed. You can certainly tell the same story over and over, for each audience may vary and your story may be worth sharing repeatedly. All I'm saying is, when you tell it again and again, keep it spontaneous and improvisational. Then you're assured it will always come across in an entertaining way. Don't forget: If you're bored, your audience will be, too.

Same goes for telling your story for the first or the only time, too. Stay focused on the finish line, but as you build to it, speak from the heart and off the cuff as much as possible. Spontaneity is such an important part of good delivery and critical to the *"What's So Funny?"* formula. I don't know of one stand-up comic who I think is really funny who stays entirely scripted as he or she goes along. Bob Hope does, of course, but while some of his jokes may get some yuks, quite frankly, I think his delivery system is a big nothing. By contrast, compare his style to that of Robin Williams. Williams is about as spontaneous as you can get! When you're spontaneous, you're unpredictable. When you're unpredictable, you're always entertaining!

Here's another reason why your sense of spontaneity is so critical: Since the average businessperson doesn't have a ton of time to spend rehearsing stories and jokes, spontaneity can be your best friend. Rehearsal of any joke, unless it's a one-liner, can take a good deal of time—something most business professionals I know are not willing to spend. So if you want to make certain your material hits the mark, keep your content loose and impromptu.

Now, if you are one of those who insists on memorizing a joke or story, fine. Spontaneity is still an attribute you'll need, because as you tell your story, you don't want to sound like you're reciting it. You want it to live and breathe and bounce. Even memorized material can come across as fresh if your spontaneity muscles are in shape. I can always tell when someone is reciting; they seem to be thinking ahead. They are never in the "moment"; they're anticipating.

Spontaneity coupled with a good energy level promises good delivery. So as you rehearse your scripted jokes and stories, you want to make them sound like those thoughts are coming into your head for the first time. I know this isn't always easy for the business professional. That's why I sell the idea of "beat points" that lead to the capper, because they take the stress off trying to remember the material and execute it at the same time. This allows you to have fun as you share colorful moments. Of course, it also relieves the pressure. I would much rather not have such a burden when I'm presenting; on the contrary, I would like to enjoy myself.

One last thing on this point: Many people who take my "What's So Funny?" class are not hysterically funny people, but as I mentioned earlier, everyone has a great ability to tell a story to another person. And staying in a spontaneous mode more closely matches the style with which you share stories with friends and trusted associates. That's when we're at our entertainment best! Remember, I'm not asking you to become a stand-up comic; I'm only asking you to invite humor and good storytelling into your speeches and presentations. If you keep your material fairly spontaneous, your stories and jokes will always work. And, once again, because staying spontaneous takes the pressure off, it will make it easier for you all around.

Some exercises that promote spontaneity include rattling off information on a subject as quickly as possible without stopping but to take a breath (it keeps the mind creative and inventive); picking a subject you know nothing about and making up a speech about it on the spot; playing a challenging but fun game of charades with friends; and lastly, my favorite, picking up an object—a rolling pin, for instance—and making up a TV commercial about it, only suggesting that it is anything but a rolling pin. After you've whizzed through a quick one-minute commercial, burst into a jingle if you're up to it. Another idea: Randomly flip through a dictionary and pick a word. Quickly make up several sentences with that word in it. What you want is to not think, to just go with whatever comes into your mind. Doing these exercises is a great way to build some self-trust, by the way. So let your mind lead you. Don't monitor, plan, control, or analyze your thoughts, just "be here now," a term we use constantly in our workshops.

Improvisational comedy is my area of expertise, and the heartbeat of that work is spontaneity. If you can take an improv-comedy class or workshop, do so; it's a wonderful way to build your skill level in the spontaneity department. Should you be unable to do so, I want you to remember one basic tenet I teach all my students: React and respond to the last thing said, or last idea held. Always. This will really keep you in the spirit of spontaneity. As I conclude your homework assignments in this area, let me also suggest that you rise to the unexpected on the job as often as possible. You'll note that there is no script at the office; everything is improvisational. Therefore, the workplace is a wonderful way to hone your spontaneity muscle. Welcome those moments of the unexpected and handle them without thinking. Just react. It will sharpen your spontaneity muscles in no time at all! Soon, you'll find it easier to tell those stories and share those jokes during your speeches and presentations more extemporaneously.

IT'S NOT WHAT YOU SAY BUT HOW YOU SAY IT

The elements we're combining to concoct our magic formula are all basics that I spend time on when teaching improvisational comedy. And believe me, no one fundamental is more important than the one I call self-expression. What the term means is you must put meaning behind the words you speak.

The sure-fire way to do that is through what ExecuProv terms mood variance, or the use of varied emotions. When we tell a story or a humorous anecdote, it must be told with feeling.

Without a well-developed "emotional vocabulary," we once again run the risk of bottoming out, mainly because everything we say sounds the same. What may have been a very funny bit might not be funny at all, simply because an appropriate emotion wasn't underscoring our words. Perhaps there was no particular mood present; without feeling, it's very hard to put a humorous point across. So the feel in your delivery has a lot to do with the success of your material.

I'll give you an example: If you were to say, "...then the punchbowl fell on my foot and I instinctively kicked it across the room," without a certain feeling when saying it, it would be as flat as the words laid out on this paper, but...if you say the same sentence in any one single mood, you would give life to the line. For instance, if you spoke with a feeling of panic, or disbelief, or sarcasm, resentment, enthusiasm—the line would stand a good chance of evoking a response from your audience. Emotion gives life to the words!

What's truly magical is when you combine two or more emotions in the same sentence. Like this: (Disbelief) "The punchbowl fell on my foot...(Pride) So I instinctively kicked it across the room." When you get really good at this principle, you'll want to try using a mood that is incongruent with your words: (Boredom) "I had such a great time, I can't wait to go there again." Though you may not have realized it before, with many successful comics (such as Bill Cosby, Paul Reiser, Jerry Seinfeld) their stuff very often has a mood behind it contrary to what they're saying. Therein lies one of the secrets to humor: Things that don't fit together make us laugh! It's just one more part of the formula and one more trick up the pro's sleeve.

To improve your emotional vocabulary, start by listening to *how* you tell your jokes and stories. Do you put meaning behind those words, or do you hold back? Observe others. Do *they* have feeling in their delivery? Make a list of ten sentences and say each one of them in at least 50 different moods.

Stretching your emotional muscles is a great work-out for making certain the appropriate mood spontaneously bolsters your words as you go about your speeches and presentations. Again, it is not what you say but how you say it. Know that as you do your regular emotional workouts, you're conditioning your subconscious to call up the right mood at the right time. Just like your stage skills, with enough practice, you won't have to think about it. But practice you must, just like the professional performer.

Can you begin to see how the first three components work together? Energy as the base, creating a spark from which spontaneity is made possible, enriched by putting meaning behind what is being spontaneously shared. To illustrate further: If we took the sentence about the punchbowl and delivered it with a reasonable amount of energy, then continued on, ad libbing about what transpired after the bowl was kicked across the room—and did all of this by attaching the various feelings that were experienced in the process—we have the beginnings of a great delivery. But let's move on, now, to the last two parts of the formula—two very important components.

TIME AND TIME AGAIN

Most comics will tell you there is nothing more crucial than a good sense of timing to execute a good joke. Without it, your material will probably miss the mark. Again, it's not what you say but how you say it, and the rhythm with which you release each word and phrase. We need pauses in all the right places. We need to build momentum as we tell our jokes and stories, incorporating interesting pauses along the way. Some lines are delivered slowly for impact, while others are blurted out in machine-gun fashion. Others find a particular cadence somewhere in between. It is the knowledge of what timing is appropriate where, and when, that is key to the delivery process.

I believe that each of us has our own sense of rhythm that is natural to us when we tell a joke or story. And that's the point I want you to pay close attention to: what your pace is—where you pause—when you speed up—that equates to your own sense of timing. For instance, when with friends and those with whom you're comfortable, you often share information in a story-telling mode, or, information of a humorous nature. That's when our timing tends to be most natural and at its best.

There is no one "right" type of timing; we each have our own blueprint in this regard. But we each have an interesting sense of timing that seems most evident when we're in situations where we feel comfortable sharing information. It could be a juicy piece of gossip, or the recollection of an incredulous experience (that didn't seem funny at the time), but each of us has a rhythm to our "speak." I want to ask now that you begin to listen to your timing when you tell someone about a personal experience or pass on some interesting information. My students often tell me that they were not aware they had such a thing as timing in their speech. It never really occurred to them. But when they listen, they soon discover it. Soon you'll identify *your* own phrasing and begin to appreciate how valuable it is to you. Next, I want you to consider how you can use this as part of your delivery style in your speeches and presentations.

To practice your sense of timing, do things that require keeping time, such as dancing, playing a sport (tennis is a great one), singing, reciting, or reading poetry aloud. Just sit and snap your fingers to music—anything along these lines will put you in touch with, and improve, your sense of timing.

After gathering more awareness of your timing, make a point of sharing a recent experience with a co-worker or friend; notice your rhythm as you deliver the information. It's probably going to become part and parcel of your style. It's an element you'll develop along the way, and, as you do, you'll come to appreciate yourself as a great performer—and one who can easily tell a good joke or story.

Another assignment I want you to take seriously is this: Study some of the great stand-up artists and their work. My personal favorite is George Burns. I think he had the most impeccable sense of timing that ever was. If you'll note, he was pretty laid-back—a straight-man, too. But whatever he said was funny because his pauses were in all the right places. He held back certain words and phrases ever so slightly. He wasn't a nano-second off his perfect phrasing; it was always right on the money. Consequently, everything he delivered worked. He was a master. Make a list of people whose timing you have come to enjoy. Study them. This assignment will be one of the most meaningful in terms of helping you ensure "killer" delivery.

THERE'S A TIME AND A PLACE FOR EVERYTHING, INCLUDING ATTITUDE

The last of the five components that assure humorous delivery and good storytelling is attitude. Now, this is not to be confused with self-expression. Emotions are meant to punctuate and give meaning to words as they are spoken. Attitude is an underlying vibe or tone that encapsulates the joke or story.

Let's return to our punchbowl example to illustrate this point. We'll continue with expressing disbelief and pride for the first and second half of that sentence, but now let's add an overall attitude to the mix. Let's say, for example, that the overriding tone is one of irritability. Yes, what you're expressing is disbelief at the bowl falling on your foot, and a sense of pride as it's kicked across the floor, but underneath all that and all that came before and after, is a permeating attitude of irritability. And, when you combine an underlying tone of irritability with a feeling of disbelief, it enriches and enhances the meaning of your story. When you continue, expressing a sense of pride atop that irritability—once again, you've given more dimension to the overall statement and it becomes even more interesting and rich.

Attitude is something that should prevail throughout any joke or story. If, for example, I was making a speech and sharing a story about my teenaged son, my overall attitude might be one of resignation. This tone would prevail in and around and underneath my telling of the story. Attitude is the storyteller's overall state of mind. Sometimes it's presented subtly. Sometimes it overrides and becomes the focal point of the delivery.

I'll give you another example: If you watched *Mad About You*, and witnessed the overall attitude of Paul Reiser's character, you probably sensed that that attitude was one of neuroticism. Granted, the words he spoke and the emotions he presented may have been different, but the overall tone was one of neuroticism. We saw this in his body language. Heard it in his tone. Saw it in his furtive movements and on his face. Conversely, if you're a *Seinfeld* fan: Jerry was often very blase, and that tone seemed to underscore the theme of his delivery in most episodes.

As I've said before, you hadn't thought much about attitude while watching your favorite comedians (or even dramatic performers). You found them effective in terms of delivery, but may not have known why. Again, I'm breaking it all down for you so you can master the pro's techniques.

You've often heard actors ask: "What's my motivation?" Well, what they're really asking is, "what attitude should I adopt with my delivery in this portion of the script (or scene)?"

So, as you go about doing your homework, begin to observe attitudes in others. Most people will not openly tell you what they're feeling or announce their state of mind, but their subtext is evident. You can detect it if you observe closely. You should also pay attention to your own attitudes, and to how many times your frame of mind changes in the course of a day. We all have distinctive points of view about many things as we react to them.

As you go about the task of telling stories and jokes in your speeches and presentations, you'll want to remember to change your "attitude" with each story, each joke. Without an underlying tone, your material can seem dull or simply flat or maybe even contrived. Professional comedians and actors are always pinpointing and implementing attitude—it's the mainstay of their routines.

THE SUM OF THE PARTS

You now have a pretty thorough understanding of what you need to deliver good stories and what it takes to get humor across. This five-part formula is essential to making sure your delivery is consistent. So, as you go about practicing each one of the five elements, resolve to work hard at them; you'll find it rewarding each time you make a speech or presentation.

To recap: You want energy to drive your material and serve as the spark to trigger spontaneous thoughts. You want to combine these basics with a good measure of self-expression and feeling as you tell your jokes and stories. In and around all this, you want your timing to enhance your spoken words— you want to surprise people; you want your timing to help build your stories and jokes. And, of course, put all these together with an undercurrent of attitude, and you have all the right ingredients to put your material across in a most effective way—whether it's humor you wish to impart, or just one great story.

I can't stress enough the importance of doing all the exercises and drills I've prescribed, for, as in any other field of endeavor, working at each step in the formula will help you build confidence and skill. Besides, I want you to really get in touch with the science of entertaining—because in the end, consistent effective delivery takes more than just talent if you want to be on the mark each and every time.

Let's move on now, taking our formula to the next level: Showing you how to use it, together with some valuable secrets of delivery.

Chapter 5

REAL FUNNY: SECRETS OF DELIVERING HUMOR

Now that you've gotten the five-part formula under your belt—understand how important energy, spontaneity, self-expression, timing, and attitude are—it's time to talk about the actual delivery of your material. Because so much of delivery has to do with item number four, timing, that is where we'll start.

TO THE BEAT OF A DIFFERENT DRUM

I've already mentioned that each of us has our own sense of rhythm when telling a story. Your job in the last chapter was to listen to your own particular rhythm when conveying an interesting piece of information—in order to get a better grasp on your own unique timing. If you listened carefully as you went along, you began to notice where you tend to pause, how you build to the finish, and how you create momentum as you worked toward that finish.

I'm almost positive that up until now, you had never even noticed those pauses.

In the business of comedy, we refer to such pauses in our timing as "beats." Very often, when you see a joke written out, or a comedy scripted with dialogue, you'll see a stage direction in parentheses that says: (beat). What the writer or director is attempting to get the actor to do is stop and count. One beat equals approximately a count of "one-one thousand." The actor counts (pauses), then he proceeds. If the writer or director wanted a longer pause in order to perfect the appropriate timing, he might write (beat-beat), and so on. He might give these stage directions in the middle of sentences, before or after them, even in the middle of words. It just depends on how he thinks the humor will best be captured.

Now, some actors come upon their own "beats" quite naturally, simply because they've been doing comedy for so long that they're very much in touch with their innate timing mechanism. Others, though, need written signposts along the way in order to execute a certain passage of dialogue exactly the way a writer or director envisions it—the way the writer or director knows it will work.

If you watched Tom Hanks in *In A League Of Their Own*, you may have noticed his impeccable timing as he played the role of the baseball coach. The line I most remember is one he delivered after making exasperated facial expressions when one of his players was crying. Hanks stopped—stared—and then said: (beat) "There's no crying in baseball!" Now, had he just blurted out that line as the girl began to cry, you, as an audience member, probably would not have laughed. We don't laugh when timing is rushed, missing, or otherwise off the mark. Granted, Hanks had all the other four elements intact: energy, attitude, self-expression, and a sense of spontaneity, but it was the sudden pause after all the facial contortions and then the delivery of the line that provided the humorous lift and finally, the punch.

Another wonderful example of a professional's perfect beats is when Jack Nicholson walked through the waiting room of his psychiatrist's office in the film *As Good As It Gets* and—after a couple of comedic pauses (beat-beat) said just that: "Have you ever considered that this is as good as it gets?" (beat), he exits. Nicholson held for a two-count before speaking, and held for one after, before continuing his brisk walk.

SKIPPING MORE THAN JUST YOUR HEART

Sometimes skipping beats altogether also works. Such was the case in *Bowfinger* when Steve Martin confronted his starlet lover because she had been sleeping with everyone involved in his prized movie—her way of clawing her way to what she perceived to be the top. He abruptly pulled her aside and said something about their relationship being over as he accused her of sleeping with the production assistant: "You slept with so and so," he said. She quickly responded: (beat) "So?" He fired back right on top of that line: (no beats, or perhaps a "quarter-note" beat) "I see what you mean, I never thought of it that way. See you tonight?" She said "Yes." He said, "Eight o'clock."

The delivery in that sequence *purposely* lacked full beats in order to assure the comedic timing. The point is this: Every piece of dialogue—every joke—every story we tell—provides choices about where we include or exclude beats in order to get to the comedic punch. For example, looking again at *Bowfinger* there were times when both Steve Martin and Eddie Murphy lingered with many beats before delivering a line, in an attempt to escalate and build to the punch. Each actor makes those choices, and so will you.

Paul Reiser's work is full of skipped beats because that's what works for him. Think of his TV commercials for AT&T long-distance phone service, as well as his work on *Mad About You*—in both cases, his idiosyncratic timing is quite evident. There are others who use beats or forego them in memorable ways. Who are they? Make a list of your own, then watch these performers in action. This is a very valuable learning experience. Nothing like analyzing the pros. Nothing like understanding how successful people come upon those laughs.

RULES OF THE GAME

As you go about delivering your "lines"—scripted or not—you will need to be mindful of where you put your beats or where you go without them. When I teach my ExecuProv students the rules in the "What's So Funny?" class, I remind them that they have to always put "air" (a beat or two) before and after each punchline—the punchline being the piece of dialogue you're building up to, the one that finishes off your story or joke. If you give it this "air," you automatically signal your listeners that your punchline is coming—and give them a moment to digest the humor before moving on to the next portion of your speech or presentation. I tell my students to think of their punchline as an island. "It's out there all by itself," I tell them. "There's nothing around it. Nothing in front of or behind it."

So then, if you're trying to perfect your timing, or get more in tune with what good timing is, think about "beats" and "air"; they are two very simple yet critical rules to excellent delivery. Dropped in at strategic places, they always work. In fact, I know comics who, as they test-drive their material in clubs, play around with where they put their beats just to identify where the strongest punch is.

THIRD LINE FROM THE START

There is a very fun improvisational comedy piece called "sitcom" that several improv groups do, including my own group, the Orange County Crazies.

We get a premise (or set-up) from the audience—basic parameters, such as who, what, and where. Then the audience is instructed to laugh at every third line, no matter what it is. Whichever actor delivers that third line (and he never knows what line might be appropriate until he hears the line before it) is asked to deliver it not only with "air" before he says it, but with more volume and a tone of finality. (These last two items, I'll cover in more detail shortly.) It works every time. The audience cracks up because they know that the third line isn't necessarily hilarious at all; it just sounds hilarious due to the way in which it is delivered. The piece proves that hitting your punchlines just right—with "air" and "beats" (and a little more volume—whether it's the funniest aside in the world or not)—is a wonderful way to ensure that your material will come across as having humorous intent.

Putting to work little secrets such as this is a terrific way to get in touch with, and create, timing—one of the most powerful tools you can use in order to nail your delivery consistently as you go about sharing your stories or jokes. But it all has to do with commitment. It's paramount that you make the decision that no matter whether the punchline is hilarious or not, you will deliver it with bravado and conviction. One of the greatest performers of all time, the late Phil Hartman, used to say, "If you believe it, they'll believe it." And, he was right. If you're committed to hitting that punchline with verve, the audience will almost always go along with you. There is something about intent that convinces the listener, as well as cues them for an appropriate response. Conversely, if you deliver a punchline meekly and without total commitment, the audience will mirror that lack of confidence right back at you.

Here's something else I want you to be mindful of: If you hold back, you can't be "in sync" with yourself. What I mean is you will find yourself out of your natural rhythm state. Whenever we're self-conscious or uncomfortable, it is hard to be spontaneous. If we don't go with our own flow it's rather difficult to ensure good timing. And once again, it's timing that ensures good delivery.

WHAT'D YA SAY?

As alluded to in the last section, one of the other interesting ploys used by the comedic actor or stand-up comedian is to always make sure that the last line (punchline) is delivered with more volume and energy than any of the lines that preceded it, as in the case of the improvised "sitcom." The mere power of more energetic force (which can be accomplished by turning up the volume of your voice) is, often enough, the way to ensure that your final line will work.

I know many stand-up comedy-students who, when they're just starting out, focus on the last line only. They forget about the build, and instead just concentrate on getting to that final line, which they're careful to blurt out with lots of volume. For them, hitting the mark eventually becomes natural because they work on conditioning themselves to "read" or "see" ahead of where they are; once they get there, that's where the emphasis is placed.

This is not to suggest that these students' stuff comes across as canned or stale—they've just trained themselves in one more way to effectively tell a story. They tell me that as they get to their final point—the last line—they stay focused on incorporating their "beats" and then hitting that final line *hard*. More loudly! More boldly. With flair. Intensity. Soon, as they concoct their stories (even if they're improvising on stage), that inner mechanism takes over, they tell me—that intuitive sense of punching the right lines in the right places at the right time.

THAT'S IT!

One more way to help with the delivery of the punchline is to think about saying that ending—that punchline—with a tone of finality. What hurts many a performer—both comedians and speakers—is that they leave the audience hanging on that last phrase or line without any sense of closure. Whatever the line, it needs to be said with certainty and a sense of "the end!" Otherwise, the audience is still waiting for the pay-off; they're sitting there expectantly thinking there is something more.

I'm sure that you never thought about "finality" as a component in executing a punchline before, but it's crucial. Here's a wonderful homework assignment: Watch a handful of sitcoms. You'll begin to notice that some of the "exit" lines you laugh at are not actually all that funny when you stop to analyze them ("exit" being lines that end the scene, or literally spur someone to make an exit). You'll begin to see that it's simply the finishing "touch" with which the actor says such lines that makes you realize such declarations or questions or statements *are* the punchlines. In most cases, it's something in their tone that suggests "it's over." So in addition to your "beats," your "air," and your "volume," now add a measure of "that's it" as you say that punchline.

ACCENTUATE THE, WHATEVER

One more method for getting your delivery to work is to emphasize certain words. When we exaggerate words, we also create timing and spice up how our stuff comes across. Think of Rodney Dangerfield's classic tagline: "I get no respect." In that sentence, he tends to put more emphasis on the word "respect" than on the other words. I also recall John Belushi's classic delivery of "...but, NOOOOOOO!" Of course, he spiked the word "no" to provide comedic value. It always worked. In another classic *Saturday Night Live* bit, Dan Ackroyd and Steve Martin were simply standing on stage looking skyward and repeating back and forth: "What the hell is it?" What made it funny was that they kept putting the emphasis on a different word each time they made the remark. "What the hell is *it*?" However they said it, it was hilarious, so long as they emphasized one of the words. "What the hell *is* it?", "What the *hell* is it?" "*What* the hell is it?" If I recall properly, the twosome just kept bantering that same identical line back and forth—with the use of no other dialogue—until the scene was over. As you will note, through the interchangeable emphasis of different words in that one line, both the meaning and the comedic intent changed. So there are many opportunities to secure a great delivery by simply putting emphasis on particular words.

Here are a couple of examples of all the tricks you can use to improve your timing:

"My boss wasn't so offended at my suggestion that we trade offices (beat). He was just a little flipped out the next Monday morning when (air) he caught me with my feet on top of his (emphasis) *desk*" (air). It wouldn't have been so (emphasis) *bad* but (beat, beat) it happened just as I was shoving my wife's photo in (emphasis) *his* wife's picture frame. (air) "Well," I said as I looked up in horror (beat, beat, beat), I can't (emphasis) *meet* with you right *now* because (beat then instant switch to a more submissive demeanor and rapid-fire delivery) I have to get back to my desk."

Or consider this simple one-liner: "...then he said (beat) I (emphasis) *hope* you can make it to the next (emphasis) *millennium...*" and I said, (beat) "hell, (air, then volume and emphasis) *I* hope I can make it to next (emphasis) *week*!"

You can take either of these examples and change the "stage directions" to get a different delivery. It doesn't matter. What does matter is that your "guideposts" occur at strategic places—at pivotal junctures—places that feel most natural and comfortable for you. Remember that sense of "rhythm" we talked about earlier.

HALF THE FUN IS GETTING THERE

We've covered the tricks and secrets to executing a punchline. But how do you get there? What is the secret to creating and keeping audiences' interest while you make your way to various comedic junctures and, ultimately, that final climax? Well, the trick is something we call "build."

In order to reach those final destinations with success, you have to establish a momentum from the very beginning of your story or joke and keep increasing this momentum as you go along. It's what we call "driving" the story or the joke. It has to do with intensifying your delivery. Now, this is not to say that you have to get louder or more emphatic with every sentence; it simply means you have to generate more interest for your audience.

"How can I do this?" you ask.

There are several ways. You can gradually and appropriately increase your energy—your output. You can also accelerate your pace. You can heighten your mood. Any of the above, singularly or in combination, can help you achieve "build."

Whatever your choices, you want to make certain you're moving your piece forward and taking the audience with you. Think of a train chugging up a hill. At first, it starts to move, then it builds some steam and soon it's pushing with great force as it makes its way to the top. Driving your story or joke is much the same. Another analogy: If you were cooking, you would start off with a simmer and turn up the heat until you reached the boiling point. It doesn't matter *how* this concept resonates with you. What matters is that you relate to "build" in some way. And to recap: Build is simply a matter of establishing momentum from the get-go, and building on it—*not letting up*—until you reach the end of the ride.

One of the most crucial aspects of a good joke or story is the way in which the "deliverer" goes about it. If the delivery has a sense of inertia, you can be darn sure the punchline won't fire. We need to build, incrementally, in order to give our outcome meaning and excitement. It's the single most important vehicle to help us reach our final destination. So, in the end, think of "build" as a rocket booster. No booster, no bang.

This is why when we teach the stand-up comic the mechanics I'm teaching you, we have them spend weeks just playing with the "build." We tell them to forget the punchline for the moment—"Don't even tell it," we say. "Just tell us the part building up to it." One of the stand-up comics I most appreciate, as I've already mentioned, is Paul Reiser. He has a wonderful way of telling a story, any story. If you've ever watched him, you'll notice that he gradually and effectively builds a ton of momentum as he reaches his punchline. He starts out in a nice, energetic mode, however—something else I want you to notice about him and other successful storytellers. They are alert, alive, and ready to tell a story. You need to prepare yourself (with warm-ups, perhaps) to be in that same place as you take to the spotlight, too.

So, as you stuff those tricks and secrets away—the ones the really good story and joke tellers use—add "build" to the mix. (Granted, "build" is not something to come upon easily when you're telling a one-liner, but with a story that has a beginning, middle, and an end, it must be an integral part of your delivery mechanics.)

IN YOUR OWN WORDS

Another secret to making your stuff work is conveying a sense of authenticity, which we come upon only when we're spontaneous. So the trick is this: If you're going to write out a story or a joke, learn it verbatim and get your "beats" in all the right places. Make sure you rehearse it. It should work every time you deliver it during this rehearsal. Videotape your rehearsal. Play it back. Does your delivery work every time or only sometimes? If your answer is the latter, you may want to move those beats around for better comedic impact. If it works every time, leave it alone. The old adage about not fixing something unless it's broken is in full force when it comes to comedy. If instead of writing down your story or joke, you're just going to wing it (which I think is the better choice; I realize you don't have enough time to memorize and rehearse), practice in front of the camera as well. If that's your choice (and it is with more than ninety percent of my students) opt for the wing-it route. The trick is just to go from beat to beat (beats, in this instance, meaning the pivotal points that tie the story together), examining whether or not you stay on track. Yes, please improvise, but don't forget to maintain continuity in terms of the subject matter in each "chunk" of story. Make an outline if you wish and just improvise within its framework.

In either instance, rehearsed word-for-word, or just improvising, notice if your delivery is consistently effective. If not, try and break it down. Explore why it's inconsistent. Could it be that sometimes when you tell your story or joke, your energy is lacking? Is there little or no self-expression? Are you "trying" rather than "being," thus losing your sense of spontaneity? Is there no undercurrent of attitude? Is your natural (what works for you) timing off? Is there no "build"? Are you just plodding along?

If you can identify what's lacking, you can easily fix it. And, I guarantee, outside of really bad material, difficulty with one of the aforementioned is usually the problem. But, hey, that's what this book is mostly about: helping you demystify the variables of good story and joke telling.

My ultimate objective is that you can begin to look forward to injecting good stories and humor into all your presentations—not just some. What's equally important is that you're comfortable doing so. In the end, it's my goal for you not only to understand, and appreciate, why your jokes and stories suddenly fire, but also to truly look forward to, and even enjoy, sharing them.

One final note: Don't forget, that as you would with anything worthwhile, you need to spend the time and effort it takes to learn your new skills. So while you're investigating why and how good delivery affects storytelling and humor remember to set aside time to do your practice assignments along the way. Good comics do and so can you. Even Mark Twain, the consummate storyteller, "worked" his stuff before presenting it!

FUN HOMEWORK

The following are a few terrific homework assignments to sharpen and hone your delivery and expand your creativity:

1. Stand in front of the mirror (or videotape yourself) and make up a story, using the following sentences as the first lines. I don't even care if you end these stories with a punchline; I simply want you to get your creative juices going:

   A. "Well, there was this huge mix up in the mail room and..."

   B. "I never meant for this to happen but I popped open my briefcase and..."

   C. "Let me give you five good reasons why I hate the word "millennium. First..."

   D. "The person who had the most influence on my career and always made me laugh was..."

   E. "So, I'm on this business trip and it seems like I'm standing there forever waiting for the luggage carousel to start dumping luggage, when suddenly..."

   F. "It's my turn to get up and make my speech but..."

   G. "So, the last time I took everyone in the office out to lunch, here's what happens..."

To offer a little assistance, I'll provide an example for one of the above. I'll choose "F," just for fun!

"It's my turn to get up and speak when suddenly... I hear this horrible noise. The sound of cloth ripping. My suit pants were a little tight, I must admit. It was shortly after the holidays, and I had eaten far too much... Let's just say: fudge was the least of it. Anyway, I'm now fully aware I've shredded the seam in the fanny of my pants. So, I smile anyway. After all, I'm wearing a long jacket. And I know if I make a beeline for the lectern, I probably won't be found out. I do it. Actually, I sort of walk backwards from the table where I was seated to the lectern. Sort of that 'keep smiling at them like you're trying to stay engaged and not break your connection.' Little did they know. Though I'm speaking now, in the back of my mind I'm devising ways—planning creative ways—to make an undetected exit. I'm also constantly pulling my jacket (20 percent stretch) further down, to ensure I'm not exposing myself. Well, when Q&A wound up the evening, I became increasingly more anxious. But people were tired. One guy kept asking me a ton of questions. The others began to exit. I smiled and waved at them as I continued answering this guy's questions. Soon it was just the two of us. I asked him to lead the way as we began to exit the room. I pretended like I didn't know how to find the parking structure. He excused himself on the way out, to use the restroom. I waited till he made the turn, then I ran all the way to the car. As I got in it and sat, I heard yet another rip. When I pulled into the garage, I immediately took my pants off and ditched them in the trash barrel. When my husband caught me as I came through the door, and asked in horror if I had delivered my speech in just high heels, panty hose and a jacket, I told him the story. We laughed till we cried. I wear only iron-clad, loose-fitting suit pants to all my speeches now."

    This was a fabricated story, but an exercise in flexing my creative muscle to finish the phrase. Now you do the same for "F," as well as all the others!

2. Select a fun story from your work-related experiences, stand in front of the mirror (or before a trusted friend or family member) and tell it, giving it as much of a humorous spin as you can. In other words, focus on the ridiculous parts of the outcome of a professional disaster, or your thoughts or feelings about a business crisis as it was happening to you. You can retell an instance at work (when you were an innocent bystander) that was bizarre, interesting, or funny. (Don't forget to keep the "build" in mind.) Again, give us your take on the situation. If at all

possible, record these either on audio or video tape. The playback is most helpful. You'll discover what's working for you and what isn't.

3. Take the following sentences and simply add one phrase or a second sentence that is a punchline. Don't *try* and make them funny. Just have fun with them. And be as spontaneous as you can be:

   A. "So, when I get to the elevator, the door opens and..."
   B. "He always does the funniest things at his presentations. Like, just last week, he held up a sign that read..."
   C. "My one philosophy about the workaholic is this..."
   D. "I'll never forget what I said when I suddenly blanked out at my first presentation. I said..."
   E. "It was the biggest mistake of my career and I remember thinking at the time..."
   F. "So as everyone in the meeting was sitting there bickering over the budget, I finally jumped up and shouted..."
   G. "Let me tell you what I'd say to Bill Gates if we were face to face. I'd say..."

   Once again, let me provide an example just to illustrate. I'll take "E". "It was the biggest mistake of my career and I remember thinking at the time...well, so I'll never work in this town again. Fine, I'll just move to Boise and take in ironing."

4. Take the sentences from exercise 2 and add one or two other choices to each of them.

5. Take your favorite sentence and punchline from above and see if you can identify where the "beats" should go, where the "air" belongs, and what words you would intensify or emphasize to give your delivery a comedic tone. Also, identify where added volume might enhance your delivery. For instance, let's take suggestion G: "You know what I'd say if I were face to face with Bill Gates? I'd say, 'Hey Bill, how about a small loan, like $20 million'." Okay, here it is with guideposts: "You know

what *I'd* say if I were face to face with Bill Gates? (Beat) I'd say, (beat) 'Hey, Bill, (beat, beat), how about a small loan, like (air; volume) $20 million?'" If you're counting these beats and following these simple stage directions, I promise you will intone this sentence humorously. Of course, my suggested breakdown is not the only possible delivery. You could pause in other places, put emphasis on other words—it just depends on *your* approach and what works for you. What I would like you to do, however, is to try the delivery as put forth in the first suggestion, then try delivering it with the specific directions in the second take. Tape this, audio or videotape, either one, and see the nice differences.

Now, the second part of this exercise is to take all of the suggested phrases, finish them in as many different ways as you wish, and break them down with your own stage directions. Next, stand and deliver them, playing with different stage direction choices as you do so. You'll see for yourself that there is not one "right" way to deliver lines, but simply choices to be made according to what suits *your* style. Above all, have fun with this.

6. Take a particular passage from an upcoming speech and see where there might be an opportunity to add an interesting aside or quip. Play with your delivery by writing the quip down and guiding yourself with your own stage directions: where to put your "beats," where the signal for "air" should go, and what words require you to increase your volume and add emphasis. Soon you'll get a great handle on how you can take virtually any line and give it a comedic twist or humorous kick. Remember what I said earlier about the "sitcom" improv piece. It isn't the actors' third line itself that is necessarily funny, but rather the way they deliver the line. Keep experimenting until you feel comfortable with the way your punchlines and stories sound. Pay attention to your own timing as you go along. You'll soon discover your "style"—it's nearly impossible not to.

I am told by many an ExecuProv "What's So Funny?" student that a willingness to experiment and diligent practice, coupled with a playback recording of their practices and rehearsals, and studying those results, have enabled them to use humor and good storytelling in all their speeches and presentations—even the ones they didn't think required such "entertainment."

7. Part One: Take the following closing remarks and make up a story that could "build" to such scripted punchlines. As you'll see, these sample punchlines don't have to be clever or purposely funny; the idea is that even the most "plain" lines can be the cappers to any story or joke. (Just imagine how well well-written material can come across!) Keep this assignment simple. Just make up an appropriate story that would end with the following lines:

   A. "...and that's when he said: '*You* try it.'"
   B. "...give me something better to *work* with!"
   C. "...so, I'll never give *that* speech again!"
   D. "...I'll just grab his briefcase and *keep* walking!"
   E. "...because you never know what she'll do *next*!"
   F. "...so much for e-mail!"

Again, I'll provide an example just to show you one possibility. I'll take "C." "So I decide to expound on the virtues of the office supply store, Staples. I start effusively telling the audience how that store always has everything I could ever want. In fact, I continually refer to them as a positive example all the way through my 20-minute talk. Suddenly the guy who hired me yells out from the back, 'Did you know Boise Cascade is a competitor of Staples?' 'Oh,' I said, plainly. So, I'll never make *that* speech again."

Part Two: Make a list of your own punchlines, and do the same exercise.

Part Three: Take your upcoming speech or presentation and look for places to insert fun punchlines—cappers—final remarks—that provide a little fun, levity, or kick to that otherwise dry message or educational lesson. (Most speeches are designed to either educate, inform, or persuade).

As you will note with all of the above assignments, there are no right or wrong answers. That means you can't fail in any way. These exercises are simply meant to help you let go, get imaginative, and play around with your delivery as you tell stories and execute punchlines.

Take pride in your efforts thus far. Even if you haven't yet *mastered* your delivery, you've found new ways of presenting your material in a more interesting, engaging, and effective manner.

Keep practicing!

Chapter 6

A Funny Bit: The Almighty Icebreaker

You know the drill. You're at that "event"—speech or presentation—and someone starts reeling off your life's achievements. Suddenly you hear your name. Your intro is over. Oh dear, it's show time! Time to take to the lectern and begin. But how do you get started? What do you say—first?

I know people who've spent hours preparing for such events. They've diligently researched their subject; they have their materials in order; they have notes all neatly laid out to help them follow their train of thought as they go along. They actually have great moments of humor ready to fire at all the right intervals. Some (though not many) have even rehearsed their speech or presentation.

But more often than not, those who confidently take to the podium have completely forgotten that they need an opening remark. An "icebreaker." Something that will put that audience at ease, establish a bond with them, and set the tone for what's to come—especially if the tone they want to convey includes (as it should!) humor.

Ergo, the icebreaker.

A GREAT WAY TO CONNECT

An icebreaker is important in any speech or presentation, if for no other reason than to make an instant connection with the audience. For the business performer who wants that audience to know they're in for a great time, an icebreaker is even more crucial. In ExecuProv classes we ask our students to *always* offer an icebreaker, because we want them to bond immediately with the audience. We also want them to convey a specific mood—a positive and upbeat one!

Remember that old saying about first impressions…

I know many speakers who either intended to be humorous, or who *were* finally humorous, but whose first few minutes at the lectern were horribly uncertain. Sometimes they'd take three or four minutes to get rolling. Meanwhile, we, the audience, couldn't figure out what frame of mind to settle into. "Is this going to be serious or fun?" I've said this to myself at the beginning of many speeches, my own mood mentally jockeying for position. More often than not, judging by the first few opening remarks, I leaned toward "serious." And, boring!

BETTER NOW THAN LATER

I'm told by many of my students that the first few moments of a speech or presentation can be agonizing, even if they have their humor together (and readily on tap for "later"), simply because they just don't know what to say to kick things off. Stammering and stuttering—starting and stopping—a mouth dropping open with no sound coming forth: these are not uncommon "openers" for those I've coached and those I've seen speak—even the best of the best. My students confide that when such things happen to them, they immediately feel awkward, self-conscious, and, often, just plain uncomfortable.

Those feelings transfer.

Even if the performer doesn't realize it, the audience feels uneasy right along with him. It's not until the fun begins somewhere later in the speech, that the audience may begin to relax.

But at that point it might be too late to get them to respond to your humorous moments as warmly as you hoped they would. Just like the stand-up comic who starts out lackluster and slow, you'll end up struggling to "prove" yourself. The audience won't be willing to respond enthusiastically—won't be as receptive to their eventual humor—because being "funny" was not exactly that audience's first impression. Their disappointment is hard to shake.

When the beginning remarks are bland, austere, or simply uninteresting, many audiences don't trust that their experience will be enjoyable or captivating. They tend to settle in and resign themselves as they mentally prepare for the "ordinary." Even if, later on, the speaker begins to throw out fun asides, it usually takes the audience a while longer to warm to the idea that they're being given permission to have some fun. And not only do dull openers send the wrong signal to the audience; they certainly don't make for great momentum for the speaker. So much for setting the tone, and so much for first impressions!

What each of us wants in those first few moments is to give the audience a glimpse of what's to come. We want to engage them, win them, bond with them, and, more than anything else, let them know they're in for a treat!

I bet you're not disagreeing with me in the least. But how do you come upon an icebreaker? Well, first let's talk about what constitutes one.

THE ANATOMY OF AN ICEBREAKER

An icebreaker is a remark, comment, statement, question, story, shared personal experience, or expressed thought that is spoken just *before* you begin your speech or presentation. It's the first thing that comes out of your mouth as you address your audience. Most often, an icebreaker is something unexpected. It's unpredictable. It's not the typical "hi, how do you do", that the audience is used to hearing. The more spontaneous the icebreaker, the better.

I, for one, never pre-plan an icebreaker. I wait until I arrive at the "gig" and see what develops. Something may happen in the room just prior to my taking the podium that will trigger a fun aside and I may opt to share it with the audience, first thing. This aside may be something one of the other speakers has said or done. Maybe it's something about the people in attendance—something I observe in their conversation or apparent group-culture. This is where my improvisational comedy training becomes so valuable. I try to "be here now"—stay in the moment—and let the many variables unfolding around me dictate how I'll open a speech or presentation. Sometimes I even wait to decide until I'm in place facing the audience. I've learned to trust myself. I've come to know that I will be appropriate. Chances are, the more spontaneous I remain, the funnier my first remarks will be. (For me that's very important because I'm selling the concept of speaking with humor!)

Of course, we can all provide icebreakers that are serious in nature—blurt out dramatic or profound statements—but, for our purposes, I'm suggesting that you start utilizing your humor muscle so your icebreaker will be comedic or light in nature. After all, it's humor and good storytelling in speeches and presentations that we're after in this how-to manual.

Another way to think about the icebreaker is to think of it in terms of "small talk." This is not to suggest that your opening remark be trite or meaningless; it's simply to point out that most of us start conversing with others by means of casual remarks. Icebreakers are the same idea: Small talk, the dialogue that helps us get acquainted with others and make that initial connection. And such remarks are not *only* introductory in nature. Think of those times on the elevator when you turn to the person next to you and say something like: "This thing is slower than my 16-year-old getting out of bed on a school day." Such "openers" help you start the conversational ball rolling.

Most of us think nothing of making small talk with strangers when there are only one or two of them. But before a crowd, or when you know the focus is entirely on you and the audience is waiting for something to happen? Forget it! It's hard enough to do the speech!

Interestingly, though, the only difference between small talk and an icebreaker is the audience. When you're making a speech or presentation, you're probably expecting the audience to return the verbal volley. But that doesn't mean that you can't do your part. If you can do it in an elevator (where, after all, the other person may just smile and say nothing), you can do it in one of those hotel banquet rooms, too!

PRACTICING WHAT I PREACH

I sell humor and fun in all my workshops and classes, so it's very important that my openers feature icebreakers that establish a comedic image. "Fine," you might be thinking. "I hear that, but give some examples." I will. But let me preface a demonstration of the different forms of icebreakers by noting that every situation and every group I address requires a different approach. So, it would be impossible for me to list every icebreaker I've ever used, or to provide you with a selection of types of them you could call up on the spur of the moment for your particular use. What I would like to offer, instead, are the following examples—all of which illustrate choices I have made in the past.

Don't forget: these pieces of dialogue are the very first things out of my mouth, even before I offer any introductory information regarding myself or what I'm there to talk about.

Remark: (Looking very stern—just to throw them off—and pausing as though I'm trying to gather my thoughts, then:) "If you find my speech boring, just scream out 'boring' any time you can…get a word in."

Comment: (To several guys in the front row) "I like your ties. They remind me of my ex-husbands'. They're a little too busy for me."

Statement: "Speeches are much more fun when (beat) other people are making them."

Question: "How many of you like to speak in public? (Gesturing for hands up) Can I see a show of hands? (A few are raised.) Good. Which one of you wants to take my place tonight?"

Story: "I was parking my car here at the hotel today and this valet guy comes up to me and says, 'Are you the speaker for the Project Management Institute Dinner?' I hand him my keys and proudly say—thinking he thinks I'm some sort of celebrity or something—'Why, yes, I am.' He says, 'Well, half of them didn't show up, if that means anything to you.' I wanted to yank my keys right out of his hand, get back in my car, and floor it. But instead, I lied and said, 'Oh, well, I'm so glad. Because, my goodness, I just hate playing to large crowds.' So…I do hope the *five* of you have a really good time…"

Shared Personal Experience: "You probably didn't know this about me, but I spoke in front of 240 Annapolis Naval Academy Midshipmen not long ago, and I lost my train of thought when a group of officers dressed in white suddenly entered the room. Ooooh, we're talking a whole bunch of Tom Cruises. And that was *not* good because tuning out distractions and staying focused is what my topic was at that *exact* moment!"

Expressed Thought: "I just have this horrible fear that as I stand here, I might fall off my shoes. (Looking down and holding out my arms like a tight-rope walker.) I *never* wear heels this high!"

Each of these icebreakers tends to fit my personality and the way I might come at an audience the minute I begin to address them. My intent is to let them know I'm human, I'm uninhibited, I'm vulnerable, and I'm fun. That's me. Your choices may differ substantially. That doesn't matter. There is no right or wrong in the icebreaker game. What does matter is that you send the right signal. You want to grab that audience from word one and keep them enraptured in your talk every step of the way. You also want to give them a feel for who you are and where you're going with your talk—from the get-go.

BREAKING YOUR OWN ICE

As I just mentioned, your icebreaker choices may differ widely from mine. That's okay. What's important is that you find your own comfort level as you select and use icebreakers and that you explore possibilities that suit *you*. Remember: In addition to your own individual "icebreaker style," every situation in which you speak or present has a different set of circumstances. With that in mind, you want your opening remark to fit the event and the people attending it. So I want to caution you not to try to prepare too many "canned" openers because they just might sound too pat, too scripted. An icebreaker is meant to set a comfortable tone and loosen up your audience—put everyone at ease including you. Your audience will feel even more relaxed knowing that your opening remarks were improvised and very "current."

I also believe an audience that hears a spontaneous first remark has an instant respect for the speaker; they perceive the speaker as smarter, more competent and confident. So, as you go about your "icebreaking" duties, consider how really powerful they are. And, as you go about experimenting—breaking your own ice, so to speak—see if you can stay spontaneous. Don't pre-plan an opener, wait until you get up there and then make a fitting remark. I know for some of you this may seem impossible, but I truly believe you're going to find that you'll say the right thing at the right event at the right time. Just give yourself permission to "wing it." Don't forget: the small talk concept.

ICEBREAKERS IN A CAN

Next, you can try icebreakers you've prepared. Perhaps you know exactly what the event will be like. You know the folks who are scheduled to attend. And you know the overall theme or agenda that's been planned. As you review your speech material (it's best to prepare this first), go back to the very beginning and jot down an icebreaker you think will work. This could be a remark that you know will address concerns or interests of the crowd. It could be a question that would elicit energy in the room—stimulate a back-and-forth dialogue with you and them. It could be a fun remark that introduces your subject matter.

I don't think there's any one way to prepare an icebreaker. I suggest you go with your instincts and let the material that will follow your opening dictate your choice.

ICE PICKS

Whether you ultimately decide that spontaneous or scripted icebreakers are more suited to your style, I would like to suggest that you begin playing with the whole concept of "icebreaker" by first experimenting with them in low-risk situations. These may include meetings where only a handful of people are in attendance but where the spotlight is on you. Maybe it's a speech before the PTA or your Cub Scout group. Maybe it's the introduction of another speaker or the kick-off remarks at the Monday morning staff meeting. Maybe it's your next elevator ride. The point is this: to practice at events where you feel little pressure. Later you can address that group of 100 and toss out your icebreaker with confidence—like the performer who plays to the small crowd and later to a full house.

Of course, even in low-risk settings, the notion of an icebreaker is scary to some. "It feels like I'm jumping off a cliff," one student told me recently. He was right. You do get that sensation, especially if your opener is spontaneous. After a while, though, you'll become more comfortable with the idea, and soon it will become second-nature. The other aspect of learning to play with icebreakers—the spontaneous ones at least—is that you enhance the improv skills you may need to lean on from time to time throughout any of your speeches and presentations. Whether you choose to offer icebreakers impromptu or pre-planned, what counts is learning how to offer them with comfort and ease.

CHIPPING AWAY

It's time now to begin some homework assignments that will assist you in developing and honing your icebreaking skills. Don't skip any one of the following exercises as each of them is equally important:

1. Begin to become conscious of what it is you can do or say as you first speak in front of any group—even if it's before a couple of people at a sales call. Things as simple as: "How about those Yankees?" Your awareness of off-handed opening remarks is a great first step.

2. As you make your next few speeches or presentations, note what you tend to say right off the bat. For example, are you one of those whose first words include your name, company affiliation, and the title or topic of your speech? "Hi, I'm Alice Johnson from CDA Corporation, and I'm here to talk about travel agencies and the complaints people have about them"? Ho-hum. How about preceding such customary remarks with an icebreaker. Example: "Anyone here ever go on a vacation that made them homesick?" Make a list of suitable icebreakers—the pre-planned types—to go with just one speech or presentation.

3. Take your last several speeches or presentations (or upcoming ones), and attach a scripted icebreaker to each of them. Even though you may not use them, this exercise serves as good practice to get you in the spirit of preparing them. To be thorough and to get a full work-out, sit quietly and write out icebreakers in each of the categories I introduced earlier: a remark, comment, statement, question, story, shared personal experience, and expressed thought. Create three of each. Be spontaneous. Next, prepare the type of icebreaker that takes some thought in constructing. It may take several rewrites until it rings true to you. Choose icebreakers for each of the prescribed categories—remarks that you think would be good openers to fit your subject matter and your audience. You will probably surprise yourself with how creative you really are!

4. Seize opportunities, when you have to speak or present, to allow yourself real-life, on-the-spot icebreakers. This lesson requires what I call semi-spontaneous icebreakers, because you do get just a wee bit of time to plan them. Here's how this homework assignment should be carried out: Take stock of the room and all its goings-on. Notice the mood, the surroundings, the ambiance, the people, and so on. Let your mind be playful and whimsical as you make these assessments. When you get a fun (or profound) idea, quickly jot it down on a cocktail napkin or notepad. Now, as you take to the podium or begin

speaking at the conference table, toss out the remark that came to you just a few moments ago.

5. Now for the big time! Take some deep breaths and clear your mind. The object in this assignment is to wait until it's time for you to speak before you select an icebreaker. Stay as spontaneous as you can. Look at the audience and then speak. I swear: If you dare to trust yourself, you will come out with the right icebreaker. But trust is the operative word here. And it takes time to build this skill. But if you have the courage to try it, you will, over time, build on your skill and ability to wing it over time.

I have always found that the most spontaneous openers are the funniest, the warmest—the most powerful. As I mentioned earlier: You can't fool the audience. They know when you're speaking off the top of your head and when you're too far into your head! Take some risks. What's the worst that can happen?

This assignment must be repeated as often as possible, incidentally, because I want you to build your strength as a spontaneous ice-breaker. Your ability to come upon that opener quickly and naturally is a wonderful asset and tool to utilize throughout any speech or presentation. Icebreakers are great precursors to developing the ability to improvise in and around your entire speech or presentation. Besides, bottom line: Your audience will love you!

6. Put on your director's hat and critique other people's openers—their icebreakers. Which ones do you like; dislike? Which ones work; which ones don't? Take a few notes and see if you can analyze why their stuff clicked or bombed. A great actor is a great observer, as I mentioned earlier. Learn from others' mistakes *and* their successes. Keep a journal. Keep it handy. It's a wonderful reference source as you go about preparing your own icebreakers. It's also a great warm-up exercise to review that journal as you get in the mood to put on your spontaneity hat just prior to that speech or presentation.

Here are some other ways to build your "icebreaker chops" and become more aware of how effective icebreakers can be for *any* communication situation:

1. Yes, ride an elevator and start a conversation with whoever's in it—with an icebreaker. Even if you feel like being silent, make yourself break through your inhibitions or shyness and speak.
2. Start every business meeting with an icebreaker. Don't get right to the subject at hand; start out with "small talk"—one remark will do. See if you can do this off the cuff. It really helps build that spontaneity muscle, in addition to building confidence in your ability to improvise.
3. Pay attention to others as they "small talk" with one another. This takes place in various situations and venues—those networking mixers, open houses, seminars, office parties. Watch how other people break the ice.

Enough homework for now! Let's move on and take a look at what's appropriate and what is not when using humor and good storytelling in speeches and presentations.

Chapter 7

THE FUNNIEST THING IS: ...
What's Appropriate, What's Not

Times have changed! It used to be that "politically correct" meant not making fun of someone's politics or religion. Those two categories were pretty much considered off-limits, but lots of other things were fair game. Remember that famous punchline: "Take my wife, please...?" Not that it ever sat very well with me, but I, and many other women, didn't stand up and scream "You can't do that anymore, or we'll sue you!"

Today, it seems, it's tricky to make fun of most things. Now, almost *everything* is off-limits. Remember the old-fashioned Polish jokes? Dumb-blonde cracks? Off-colored knock-knock volleys? People object, period. And in view of the new societal mindset, it's hard to poke fun at things like ethnicity, sexual orientation, gender differences (there aren't supposed to be any), handicaps (and not just the physical ones), lifestyles, professions, art forms...the list is endless!

I'm not saying any of these categories *should* be made fun of. Perhaps not. Especially if the jokes are demeaning and cruel. I don't think it's fun to mock anything or anyone maliciously. I take real issue with hurting anyone's feelings or stepping on sensitivities just for a good laugh. But, hey! Isn't everyone just a *little* too uptight these days? Haven't we gone just a little too far the *other* way? Friends used to tease me playfully—about being Italian. Well, they couldn't do that comfortably in today's world!

Of course, even if we have indeed, swung too far the other way—even if we are too uptight, too hyper-sensitive—it doesn't matter. No matter how we feel personally (and I tend to be a little more liberal—because I believe it's healthy to laugh at the craziness around us), what counts is that we adapt to what is appropriate to our audiences today. Our audiences demand that, or we bomb—we crash in the most horrible way. So then, only when we begin to understand what *doesn't* work in today's comedic economy—and why—can we move on to what does work—and how.

LOOKEE WHO

But first, I want you to take note of both the speaker and the audience member these days. As I mentioned, both are far more sensitive than they once were (because of the emphasis on "political correctness"), so it's hard for any of us to truly define what's appropriate and what is not.

If you're one of those who argues there's no point in trying to be humorous because you're bound to offend someone, I can relate. I can sympathize. It makes being funny more difficult. Because in addition to trying to develop a comedic style and presence, now you also have to be a genius when it comes to choosing what to say. If you're a professional comic and you offend someone, things are a little different: you just take your act to a different club or, as they say, keep your day-job. For the business professional, though, a joke that offends someone could mean the difference between being employed one day and unemployed the next!

Having said all that, I don't want you to be deterred by an overly sensitive society, for there are ways around it—ways to still poke fun at the world and the things in it. There are ways to make people laugh just as hard as they seemed to in the past. We just have to recognize what's okay and what's clearly off-limits. Don't ever forget what I've pointed out all along in this book: Everybody wants to laugh; they love humor, and they love a good story. You simply have to find what material to use and what to stay away from.

THE WAY WE WERE

Comedy—like anything else, I think—is trendy! And to understand that, I suggest we look back in time, if only to the past four decades. Let's start with the 50s. It was a fairly conservative decade, and, back then, humor was cute. We had Red-Skelton-type-humor—Bob Hope—*The Donna Reed Show*, and Sid Caesar's *Your Show of Shows*.

During the '60s humor began to reflect the rebellion against the '50s and suddenly we had comics like Lenny Bruce and George Carlin and shows like *Laugh In*. Comedy was suddenly getting a little "edgy," and angry.

Next, of course, came the '70s and *Saturday Night Live*. We know how many cycles that show has gone through and how its comedy choices have cleverly mirrored the world's satirical threshold through each of the show's eras. With *SNL*, comedy became a little more innovative and outspoken. Belushi and Ackroyd had a field day both as writers and performers. (We also had *Cheers*, a forerunner of what future sitcoms were to look like.)

The '80s gave us (more of) Steve Martin, Martin Short, Billy Crystal, and Eddie Murphy—some real high points for a lot of us who really like to laugh. More chances were taken, and parodies were the order of the day. Toward the end of that era came Phil Hartman. He showed us what versatility was all about, as well as comedy with class.

The '90s gave us *Seinfeld*, *Mad About You, Friends, The Simpsons*, and satirical shows like *In Living Color* and *Mad TV*. This decade produced some "smart" comedy—and socially conscious shows, too. *Ellen* clearly illustrated that.

Once you begin to study a mix of comedically-oriented shows in all these eras, you'll see change. You'll see things that were acceptable then, but I want you to ask this: Would they be acceptable today?

Which brings me to my next question: Where are we today? Howard Stern notwithstanding, I think we're headed for a more conservative groove again. If I hear one more "so and so is blankety-blank-challenged," I think I'll scream. That concept conjures up handicaps and shortcomings for *everyone,* which means that making fun of any one of them is strictly taboo.

Not much left to play with, it seems.

WHERE DO WE GO FROM HERE?

Where does this leave the business professional? Well, in terms of appropriate material, it looks like we're leaning a little more to the "right" (in more ways than one). In that case, we need pretty stringent guidelines. Before we get to what I perceive those guidelines to be, however, I'm asking that you do as I have suggested. Peruse some of the comedy of yesteryear. Take note of how times have changed—how events and situations have shaped what was, and what was not, appropriate in the past several decades in the way of generally accepted comedy material.

While we're at it, just for fun and additional insight, let's delve a bit into the last few decades and what seemed, at least in our culture, universally A-okay.

When I was a performer with the L.A. Groundlings in the mid '70s (Laraine Newman, an original Not Ready for Prime Time Player, was one of my colleagues), we made fun of everything. We had little fear about offending any audience. It seems to me now, as I look back, that folks were far less touchy. But then, in the early '80s, people started speaking out against certain social issues—like workplace sexual harassment—so some comics (not all) began backing off the dumb-blonde jokes. At the beginning of the '90s, when I started the sketch and improv Orange County Crazies company, we were pretty free with our lampooning at first. We live in Yuppie territory, and everything in the 33 cities within our county seemed fair game. Within a couple of years, however, we began to back off of certain sketches. There was "The Asian Driving School," for instance (I needn't explain; but see, I may have just offended you!). And there was "Education First" (in which a group of underprivileged high school students master math only by calculating the profit-and-loss of drug deals and prostitute tricks, equations of bullets needed for drive-by shootings, and the kicker: estimating how many illegal aliens one could fit in the trunk of a Chevy Nova). Though our audiences loved these skits—they expected us to be satirical about the realities of the day—we, along with similar sketch-oriented groups, began to pull back. The climate began to change, and groups like ours got collectively nervous about being so playfully outspoken. Suddenly every ethnic group found fault with exaggerating their idiosyncrasies. Sexual harassment lawsuits came into vogue. Gay rights were not to be spoofed. Violence became too prevalent to take a swipe at. Suddenly nothing about women's rights was that amusing anymore. And, if you picked on either gender, you were accused of "bashing." The word "abuse" was thrown around as freely as confetti.

Soon we, as well as other groups in the biz, opted for safer ground with pieces like "Hookers on Phonics," "Too Much Shoulder Pad" (in which two women confess before a support group—and graphically illustrate—how they bolstered their shoulders with items like melons and car visors as they became increasingly more addicted to shoulder pads), and "Buy A Gun, Get An Oscar." The latter, I would scratch today—I wouldn't even attempt it in light of all the horrible shootings around the country. It's one more of society's profound ills.

We also began to scale down the use of profanity so as not to offend anyone, making our shows more "G" rated. It suddenly wasn't politically correct to swear unless it was absolutely integral to the sketch (which was fine with me, since I think the constant need to swear cheapens a comic's work). And very few were taking a crack at AIDS jokes (these have always been forbidden on my stage). All in all, I don't think people were becoming more conservative, as much as they were becoming downright touchy! In our work, we have to appeal to people ages 18 to 80, and most of our audiences, even the younger ones, have become far more reserved in terms of what is socially acceptable.

To illustrate how dramatically "comedy acceptance" has changed, I want to present a couple of tasks. These will also help you better understand the "whys" in terms of material as you draw your own general conclusions about what flies and what doesn't.

1. Rent one or more videos of some of your favorite comedic performers from a couple of decades past. Watch. Then ask yourself if the humor would be acceptable to audiences today. I'll give you an example: Richard Pryor has a concert videotape that is laced with profanity—and more importantly, that trashes women in a big way. I'm not so sure today's females would tolerate such remarks. He also constantly spews out the "N" word, and I definitely doubt that would fly on today's comedic flagpole, at least to mass audiences. Make sure you study comics who commented on the society of the day, and make a list of what you think worked back then and whether it would work today. If not, list why not.
2. Listen to records and read books and newspaper columns, etc., from the '50s, '60s, and '70s, then the '80s and early '90s. Read comedic commentaries on society's goings-on. Would an Art Buchwald column of yesterday still stand today? Are such writers timeless, or would some of their work prove offensive today? You be the judge.
3. Make a list of who you found funny, and why, from the past three to four decades. Not just your favorite performers, but friends, family, business associates... Now, list the things you laughed at then: Would the comments offend you (or the audiences you might speak before) today?
4. Make your own list of tasks that will help you better understand what worked "then" and what works now. Get as creative and resourceful as you can. Think about how you might address the PTA with humor today. Would you have taken more, or less, liberty in the past? Think about other situations and groups to whom you've spoken. Make the same comparisons.
5. Keep a journal (notes) from your studies for reference purposes. You'll lean heavily on them later on. You'll be astounded at how well they'll serve as a compass for guiding you along your own humor and good-storytelling trail.

6. Jot down a few ideas about where you think society is today. For instance, can we poke fun at campaign money that is spent on presidential candidates—and make everyone laugh? Probably. But can we blast women in politics? Not as easily, I'm afraid. You can try, but I'll bet someone around you will get miffed! (Me included!) This last assignment is very important, because ***until you can get a finger on the pulse of people's issues and concerns today, you can't decipher which topics are fair game and which ones aren't.*** Knowing more about events and people's points of view in relation to them is a great way to start gathering appropriate material that will hit some very funny nerves. All that goes on in the world around us affects us as business professionals, so all the more reason to begin to bone up and take stock. Watch the news. Read the paper. Pay attention.

In the end, I think you'll come to realize that these few short assignments are key in helping you pave the way for making good, sound comedy-material choices. Again, the point is to study the shifts in comedy trends. If you pick this book up 20 years from now, the same assignments will apply. Just add another two decades on to your "review" section.

I am a firm believer that if you want to be a good humorist and storyteller you have to study what has gone before, as well as what goes on today. So, whenever you decide to do these tasks, the same principle applies. Think about then and now. Remember, we're talking trends. Remember our overall goal: to have total success infusing humor and good storytelling into our speeches and presentations. And since we're re-examining things, I want to remind you that in the previous chapters you've already begun to master your style and delivery. Now it's important to couple that mastery with material that will ensure you total success.

THE LOOK OF TODAY

My group, the Orange County Crazies, as well as other such satirical groups, have had to alter their approach with material or risk losing audience members. In our business we try to strike a balance between keeping audiences happy and not compromising our "voice" about current goings-on. If the Crazies and similar organizations have gone through their changes—i.e., if they are now opting for safety zones—you can imagine how much more confining humor choices must be for the business professional who really doesn't have the luxury of taking many comedic chances at all. I don't want to discourage you using humor at all, because it can still be done despite the restrictions. I just want to caution you that in business there is little margin for error and I don't want you to have the added pressure of wondering if, while you're trying to entertain people (with great style), the remarks you're making might offend. Better to be safe. There is always enough material that is safe.

Every humorous remark you make should be in good taste. And sometimes drawing the line is a judgment call that requires quick thinking and fast responses. So I want to see you make judicious choices with your material. Always.

FINGER ON THE PULSE

My boundaries for the appropriate use of humor in the business setting are determined by what I think the "market" will bear. In other words, I consider two things: the given audience and the given circumstances. These factors can be as diverse as the items in a garage sale.

Here's the first thing to ask about your "market": Who is your audience? Whether your material is scripted or just an outline or notes, you need to know *who* you'll be addressing and what their expectations may be. For instance, are your audience members people in your department? A potential new client? A large association? A bunch of stockholders? Whatever their category, can you anticipate what the "climate" in the room might be? What they're likely to expect?

Even if your speech remains the same, every audience will be different. Remember that. Even one additional person sitting in on your presentation might altogether change the chemistry in the room. So then, you want to get up to speed regarding who will be in the room, what their personalities are like—and arrange your "comedy mood" accordingly.

If your speech or presentation is in front of clients, you may already have a head start. I, myself, have both conservative and very liberal clients. Before I arrive at any "pitch" session I get my mind in a certain groove that's congruent with what my "market will bear." I have a group of lawyers I work for, for instance, and whenever I hawk a new promotional marketing idea to them, my humor approach is "occasional" as well as very "middle of the road".

However, with a very avant-garde CPA firm—a group that has a rather irreverent approach to things—I am looser with my comedic asides because I've come to know that's what they look forward to when I'm in the room.

When making a speech on my ExecuProv work, I also take stock of who the audience will be. For starters, I always ask questions of the person who books me. What have their other programs been like? What do they expect of me? Will the people I will be addressing be outgoing or rather subdued? I do my homework so at least I have some idea, going in, what might be appropriate. (This is not unlike the comic who plays a specific club and checks out the demographics.) But even after all that, I still wait until I find myself in the midst of the audience to begin to take the humor "temperature."

But what about those groups and clients where there is no "predict" factor? That's where my improv training comes in. I listen carefully. I do what we term: "Smell The Audience." In other words, as soon as I arrive at the scene, I pick up the vibes, assess the mood, and I intently listen to the conversations around me to get a feel for the overall mix and attitude of the group. Is there laughter in the room? A light ambiance in terms of the group's energy? Or are people restrained and inhibited? All this will guide me as I decide what jokes to tell—how far I can go—what groove I should be in to make them laugh—and, of course, what icebreaker to use. Once again, this is where the icebreaker can be so critical. (It serves as the dipstick that measures the audience's collective mindset.) Sometimes I throw out a quick opening barb just to see how ready they are to laugh. If they signal that they like my humorous approach, then I continue down that track. If they respond with silence, or I pick up only a few hesitant or random laughs, I come at them a little more gently and slowly as I dole out my humor.

My goal, always, is to let people know they're going to have a good time. So the sooner I find out how hard I have to "work" the crowd, the better. Most importantly, however, is to gauge what will be appropriate for this audience.

I let my humorous remarks mirror the existing positive energy and stimulate more of it. If I encounter a group that is subdued and less than enthused, I make it my mission to lighten them up and get them chuckling, then laughing harder. But in all instances, I never take "over the line" chances. I stay "this side" of "edgy". I am always fun, but I would never cross that invisible line. And as I have said, there is enough great material without having to risk it all!

Granted, I have lots of experience as a performer and an improv director, which means I usually know how to play off any audience—but still, I need to be very plugged in so as not to go too far.

On the other hand, though, I also strive to not hold back too much. I don't want to cheat my audience. An example: I was once asked to speak at an industry association evening meeting. The audience was saying goodbye to one president and inducting another. The outgoing officer was being teased by just about everyone who took the podium. It was a "roast" atmosphere, and when I reached the lectern, I pitched in. My remarks were teasing, too. I had taken stock of the direction in which others were going, noticed it was safe to step a little outside "typical professional boundaries," and began to play. Both I and the audience (including the guy we picked on) had a blast. So again, for all of us, finding what is appropriate depends on what the market and the circumstances will bear.

Now that you understand that it's a matter of what to supply in order to meet the demand, let's move forward to consider a few guidelines. These, I believe, will help make your material politically acceptable and show you what will, most likely, be unacceptable.

1. Stay away from any racial inferences, overtones, or cute ethnic jokes. Mimicking the dialect of someone of Vietnamese origin, for instance, isn't going to cut it. Instead,

mimic someone in your family or one of your friends—that is far less offensive and can be downright funny. I used to mimic my English-born grandfather from Sheffield. His accent was so Cockney, I never knew what the heck he was saying. But I was totally safe when I took him on because I was poking fun at my own stuff. Our own stuff—whether it's people or things—our own things are always funny to others.

2. Don't denigrate anyone: the other gender, people who have it better or worse than you, and especially children and the elderly. When we pick on others today (unless everyone is against them or what they've done—Bill Clinton's choice to have an affair with Monica Lewinsky would work because it's so universally obvious, for example), we make everyone feel nervous that someone may blow up, unless the climate is such that everyone *agrees* with your poke. Obviously you don't want to make caustic jokes about your clients or your boss, either. It just might be the last speech or presentation you make (for that company, anyway.) Putting others down is never a good choice.

3. Don't display hostility, sarcasm, anger, or resentment when telling stories or flinging humor. It just makes people feel uncomfortable and ultimately bad. These attitudes often take the humor out of good material, too. So, any display of this kind is counter-productive. The only time such negative displays are safe to use is when you're telling a story and portraying a character with one or more of these attitudes.

4. When you pick and plan the stories and jokes you will share, ask yourself how you would feel being at the other end of hearing them. Would they make you gasp? Would you be offended by them? Would you worry someone around you might be offended? Would they feel "safe" all the way around? Do the self test.

5. Watch for the checklist of things businesspeople no longer use in their humor. They include references to the sexy secretary, slamming the "different" co-worker, picking on

someone's dress. Make your own list.   Of course, there are general areas to stay away from, too. They include pro-life issues (a woman's right to choose); ethnic slurs; anything that smacks of sexual harassment; weight problems; physical or mental handicaps; jokes and comments that are too flirtatious or downright sexual; people's means, whether they are meager or exorbitant; the suburbs; people's political beliefs; people's religious preferences; and especially people's self-conscious "faults"—like someone who is going bald, someone who is obviously shorter than he wants to be, someone who has a lisp, or someone wearing clothes that are not as expensive as the next guy's.

And, for goodness sake, don't use any scatological humor—that is, bathroom humor. That is clearly tacky.

If you mistakenly throw out an inappropriate or politically incorrect comment, throw the boomerang right back at yourself as a quick comeback. An example: Maybe you've just spouted off in your speech using a quip about bald people. Maybe suddenly you spot someone in your audience who is bald—you know you may have stung them with your comment. You can (somewhat) recover by saying something like, "Well, I wish I were going bald. I'd trade that for being 15 pounds overweight and not being able to get a date in six months." The audience tends to forgive you if you paint yourself as the underdog. We tend to side with the underdog. It's also an indirect apology. (You can also apologize outright for saying what you did. But, I'm hopeful you'll never have to because you've made quick, perceptive and appropriate choices.)

6. If you're not certain about a particular joke or story, don't use it. Choose something else. Though I advocate being unique and fun, loose, inventive, and a little on the "edge," I advocate even more strongly not taking chances when the situation is marginal.

7. Don't leave anyone out of the fun. Include something for everyone. I've seen people kibitz in a board meeting with a "privileged" handful, leaving others out of the "kidding"

loop. When delivering humor and good storytelling, we need to play to the whole "house." Make certain your humor material appeals to all.

8. The most helpful—and safest—guidelines in the way of making your choices for material is to put the jokes on yourself. As I mentioned earlier in the book, when we share our innermost thoughts and feelings, we're almost always safe—so long as we don't share these at someone else's expense. A good example of sharing a personal tidbit inappropriately: "There I was in line at the bank, and these two Afro-American guys just stared at me. I got totally paranoid because all I could picture was them robbing me and stealing my car. And shoot, my groceries were in it." People will not only assume you're a racist, they'll squirm—perhaps even groan. Maybe you didn't even mean anything biased. It doesn't matter. People don't know that. They tend toward that "touchy" reaction. It's where society is today. Better to say, "There I was in line at the bank, and these two guys looked at me. They seemed rather shifty, and I wondered if they were going to rob me and steal my car. I hoped not, because my groceries were in it." If you're poking fun at a stereotype, turn the fun back on yourself. Here are a few bits I've used:

(To a banking group when first taking the podium): "I feel so out of place here. Look at all those blue pin-striped suits out there...and me in my garish peach linen. How flamboyant of me! Oh, great, now I'll never get a loan! I'll pay a hundred bucks to any one of you to borrow one of those. Ah, come on, you (pointing to one of them) give me a break, I'm sure you've got (beat) six, seven more just like it at home." Indeed, I'm making fun of bankers and their traditional three-piece, but in a way that won't make them feel bad. Instead, the joke's on me. In other words: They're okay, I'm not.

Next:

(To the Cooking Industry of America): "Cook? Forgive me if I can't relate to any of you. Heck, my children have a saying: 'If Stouffers doesn't make it, we haven't had it.'" In so many words, I'm telling them I don't feel cooking is that important, but I'm doing it in a way that won't hurt their feelings. Again, the joke is on me.

Here's another: If I'm making a speech and it's noticeably warm and uncomfortable in the room, and I don't want to embarrass anyone or all of the group, I might say: "Is it warm in this room, or am I just running low on estrogen?" Sometimes speaking for the group through comedy is a wonderful bonding experience.

As you can see, all of these remarks bounce back on me. I can have fun, but I know it won't be at anyone's expense. So, as you begin to organize and craft your humor and storytelling material—in the business setting—stay within safe boundaries. Assess the audience; know what the market will bear; make yourself and everyone else comfortable. Stay clear of any questionable content and ask yourself how you would react if you were in the audience listening to your stuff. I like this last rule because it really helps to clarify what may or may not be safe. Following it tends to keep us objective, and as a result of course, appropriate.

Now, here are a few ways to test your audience to see if your material is "room appropriate".

1. Start with a humorous icebreaker and try to assess what percentage responded positively. If the majority is with you, you pretty much know they could use more of the same. If most everyone seemed hesitant to laugh or even display a smile, then build slowly or take another tack.

2. Sense the energy in the room. Does it seem conservative, or loose and playful? A reasonable assessment of even the din in the room should help guide you. Groups tend to collect their own energy. If you listen carefully, you can hear and feel it. I know. I've seen this during shows when I'm spontaneously playing with the audience. Sometimes they mirror back the reserve of Dominican nuns; other times, I think I'm in a scene right out of *Animal House*.

3. Ask a few questions in a playful manner and see what answers you get back. Does the audience play off your remarks or are they simply not participating? If the former,

up the ante. If the latter, see if you can skillfully pull them out of their austere demeanor and get them to have some fun with you. Don't yank them abruptly. Do it gently. One way: tell them a funny story about yourself that would have meaning to them in some way.

4. Strike up a conversation with the host before you go "on." I once made a rush to judgment with a guy who looked grumpier than Scrooge. After a few moments of conversation, I realized his looks were deceiving. He was funnier than hell. Since he was booking the speakers, I felt pretty secure in starting out with some witty banter. Had I not made this attempt to "read" him, I may have missed out on all the fun—right along with the audience.

Whether your appearance calls for planned material or impromptu remarks, take the time to learn all you can about the group you're going to be addressing. This could include a small group of six or a large one of 600. Of course, sometimes it's just plain hard to get a head start in knowing what your limits might be, what your "market" will bear, or exactly what the circumstances will be. In those instances, always play it safe! Today's trend, as I've said, leans toward the conservative. Everyone has a cause, and to make fun of their rights or limitations or inabilities is, often, to offend. Be diplomatic and polite with your humor and stories. Do all these assignments as often as you need to. Don't forget: Times change!

Now, that you've gotten a handle on what constitutes appropriate material, let's move on to explore when and where you can use it.

Chapter 8

TOO FUNNY: A TIME AND A PLACE FOR HUMOR

We just discussed what is appropriate and what is not in terms of material. We also talked about what the market would bear. While the focus in the previous chapter was on the "given audience," I'd now like to cover "given circumstance:" that is, when and where you can effectively and appropriately use your humor and stories.

Even if those who make up your audience are apt to be receptive to your material, that still begs the question: Is the time and place right?

Like "given audience," the rules for "given circumstance" are not an exact science, but there are some parameters. And they're simple, really. They have to do with "you" more than "them" or "when and where." In terms of knowing the appropriate time and the appropriate place to tell a good story or share a hearty joke, what it comes down to is two things about you: your sense of good taste and your natural instincts.

Those speakers who allege, "Well, it didn't work because it just wasn't the right time or place for my joke" may have been lacking in terms of what was tasteful for the "given circumstance," or perhaps they blew off their instinct to handle the situation at a key moment. Maybe they thought things through too much. Or, maybe they did the reverse: verbally jumped the gun too quickly. These, I believe are often the *only* reasons "time and place" become a problem. Choice of material is indeed important but you have to ask: Is this a good time? Is this the right place? And then you have to respond accordingly.

The real problem, it seems, is that most people decide categorically that "it" isn't the right time or place, rather than waiting for the ideal opportunity in any "given circumstance" to slide in a joke or story, whether it's pre-planned or a spontaneous hit.

Where there is dialogue, there needs to be humor and good storytelling. This applies to both one-on-one communication, and speeches and presentations.

Which brings me to my next point.

Some may argue that I'm nuts—that I'm swinging way out there when I say this—but: I truly believe there is something appropriate in the way of a good story or a humorous aside for nearly every occasion, every "given circumstance." Shortly, I'll back up my theory with guidelines and suggestions, but in the meantime I want you to consider that, with enough finesse, you can safely provide humor or a story for just about any business occasion. I just don't buy into the notion that there are instances where you can't wedge in a little lightness, even in the heaviest of meetings. I've said it before and I'll say it again: Corporate America is just too, well, businesslike. We need balance. With all that grind, we need a little glee.

I have literally walked into a presentation (to instruct a group about the merits of improv-comedy training for the business professional) and noticed deep grooves and creases etched in the faces of upwardly mobile 30-year-olds. I have seen senior managers look like they're carrying the continent of Asia on their backs, and secretaries who are so tense and jumpy, just a supportive pat on the shoulder might cause them to ascend right through the ceiling. So, my philosophy is: each of us should look for moments—seek out "times and places"—make it our mission—to bring cheer to those around us in the workplace. We shouldn't fear—assume that—it just *isn't* the right time or the right place; for such reticence cheats all the way around. Instead, we should learn more about the skill it takes to venture forth and make our audiences—whoever they may be—feel good.

You may be saying to yourself that all this sounds reasonable, but how do you clearly define when and where it is appropriate to include humor and good storytelling? That's hard to do since every situation represents a different set of circumstances—which, incidentally, is the fundamental thing you need to understand. But what's not so hard to do is get more adroit at looking for "right times and places." When you notice them, you'll of course want to seize them!

To start the process, the first thing you want to do is to observe, be aware, stay alert and always at the ready as you scan the room and the audience, whether it's a very small group or a huge one. Next, you'll want to stay "in the moment" at all times. In other words, don't think ahead to what you're *going* to say and do, or to what they may say and do. By the same token, don't linger in the past few moments. Just stay very "current and present." That, in and of itself, as a state of mind, will help you tremendously in terms of snatching up great opportunities. We do this as improv-comedy actors every single second we're on the stage!

TIME OUT

I usually take a few moments before any speech or even a small presentation to gather my thoughts. I run down what I'll be pitching or informing the audience about. I scan my mental bank to see if, with certain ideas I'll be conveying, there might be the possibility for a bit of humor or an interesting or entertaining story. Sometimes I may just have a couple of things up my sleeve, and I implement them in strategic places—places that I think will work for the "given circumstance." Other times (and for me, these times happen often), I have to fly by the seat of my proverbial pants and instantly grab pivotal moments to spice things up. (To be more specific: These are the times I'm bantering with the audience. I remain playful as I react to what they say and do). But in either case, I'm poised like a salivating dog waiting for the doggie treat to be tossed in my direction. When the right time at the right place flies my way, I lunge for it. I want you to become trained to do the same. So then, a keen awareness and a "ready-set-go" state of mind is the prerequisite here.

This is how you get really good at instantly assessing a "given circumstance," by the way. Your responses can become laser-quick—quick enough to know that you have to pass because the time or place just didn't "feel" right. I know business speakers who are such space cadets, that they aren't even aware of their surroundings. They're simply caught up in their "agenda," so a witty opportunity may pass them by like a speeding ten-wheeler on a desert highway. But when you're in position, like a football running back, you increase your chances to wedge in a good story or a quick barb.

Of course there are caveats to all things, and as such, there are some jokes and stories that just wouldn't go over very well in a select "given circumstance." This is where you begin to rely on two of your other assets: good taste and basic instinct. The latter you're born with; the former you may have to develop over time. However, bottom line: These two fundamentals will invariably guide you as you make split-second decisions when the pressure is on. They will also serve as guideposts for that material which you pre-plan to include in a speech or presentation. For now, just remember that there are obvious "times" when you need to forego an urge to share.

For example, you certainly wouldn't want to blurt out a one-liner about the anatomy of a boss' ego if your boss were in the meeting. Nor would you want to share a good story about the humorous horrors of property-settlement agreements, amusing as they may be, in front of a client who you just learned split with his wife. And his family, and a *few* of his personal belongings. In other words, in spite of the suggestion that you strive for humor and storytelling at every "time" and in every "place," what's more important is that the material you select fit the "given circumstance," and that you're always mindful and sensitive to the people in your presence. If the material fits, then time and place become almost secondary. You simply need to find ideal moments to use such material. Which brings me back to my original point: If you have good taste and you rely on your instincts, you'll know when and where to offer humor and stories almost every single time.

REASONS TO CARE

I've said before that I like to use humor and good storytelling in every speech or presentation I give. It adds entertainment value, and I firmly believe, as I keep saying, that our job is to entertain every audience, no matter the size. I may decide ahead of time what funny tidbit to share or what amusing story to impart; then again, I may just remember a funny bit on the spot and spontaneously throw it into my monologue. But in just about every instance, I am comfortable in first considering both those basics—taste and instinct. The last thing I want to do is cross that imaginary line for I could get slammed against the wall by gasps of air or bulging eyes—both of which are usually followed by a deafening silence. And in that case, there I'd be, hoping the podium would open up wide enough to swallow me into subterranean parking.

In my public-speaking-world, practicing what I'm preaching to you is tricky because, in almost every case, it's expected that I will incorporate a fun line or a good story in my deliveries. It's my line of work; it's a lot of what I sell, after all. But, holy cow, what if my judgment is off! I might never work in "that town" again. And should I watch those sinking faces peering back at me, I may never want to. So I, too, take every precaution. The difference, however, is that I also take every chance.

What I began to do early on was develop an internal auditor—an inner voice of sorts. I did this many years ago as I first began to refine my improvisational-comedy abilities. I learned—and it's really all I learned—not so much what was appropriate, but rather when and where I should "participate." So even if you don't have the benefit of taking several years of improv classes (it's like mental boot camp), you can still develop your internal auditor and allow it to guide you.

And that's what I would like you to do next: Pay attention to that voice. It's like Diogenes with a lamp. If you listen to it, it will lead you—let you know when the "time is right." I, as I said, especially rely on my instincts in those speeches and presentations that are impromptu, because in my professional arena there is no margin for error. (Don't forget, I get paid to teach people how to tell jokes and stories "appropriately," so I can't violate the very principles I teach.) By listening to that internal voice, and following the advice I'm instantly given, I judge if it's "right time/right place."

The other component in the mix is good taste. Most of us come upon this asset by way of child-rearing or from making horribly embarrassing faux pas that we would never repeat. Now it's time to take stock of your taste and ask yourself if you're up to speed as it relates to the business community. Times have changed, don't forget, and so have the boundaries of good taste. What you may have done or said in yesteryear's time and place may no longer apply. Good taste evolves, and you need to do so with it.

I have spent a good deal of time refining my own sense and understanding of good taste as it relates and applies to the business community. The first thing to acknowledge is that "taste" in the workplace will most likely differ from "taste" among friends and family. Begin to assess where you rank in this department. Are people often blushing when you throw out a quick (what you think is) humorous remark? Do you get a subtle but dirty look? Hear a "tsk" or a "cha"? Do people look away or down, sending the signal that you picked a "very bad time?" Do some soul searching. Get your good taste "chops" up, because "time and place" is heavily reliant on your sense of choices here.

WHAT I DO

It's time to share with you what I do to keep from embarrassing myself, as well as to let you in on how I have built a sense of confidence in making good choices so that I won't say the wrong thing at the wrong time in the wrong place.

First, I get aligned with my inner sense of bravado—give myself permission of sorts to continually look for and integrate humor and stories during those "perfect" times and places. For, as I have come to see it, many people give up before they can even get started, because they are so afraid of making fools of themselves. I plan to get more explicit in describing the do's and don'ts of speech-making etiquette (or good taste, if you prefer). I'll also be more specific about ways in which to perfect your ability to rely on your natural instincts. But for now, I just want you to tap into your resolve to "go for it."

DON'T GIVE UP THE HUMOR

It's not unusual to find that some students withdraw from even attempting to wield their jokes and stories freely. I think they come face to face with the potential horror of making a mistake. They freeze up just thinking about what it might be like to be at the bad end of "wrong place/wrong time." For some, it isn't worth the risk.

If you don't want to fall into that trap—and I certainly hope you don't—you must tell yourself you're going to take chances, albeit small ones. With each success, you'll build confidence. And think about it: Without this confidence, you're going to use humor and good storytelling less and less, so what would be the point of getting all these skills in place? Tell yourself there is always opportunity in every "time and place" for your humor and stories. Take every speech or presentation and tell yourself you will find the right material for every "given circumstance," and that you'll interject appropriate material—whether you plan ahead for it or do it spontaneously. This task will aid you in building the self-assuredness that only comes from practice and concrete results. But again, be brave!

GOTTA HAVE IT

I want to sidetrack here to make a point before we go further: One of the reasons you want to conquer any fears you may have regarding time and place is, quite simply, that mastering and using your comic abilities is going to make you feel good. For instance, if I couldn't count on that "high" you get only from a live audience who expectantly waits for the next amusing moment, I probably would lose my enthusiasm for making speeches and presentations altogether. I need stimulation when I work, and nothing provides it more plentifully than the positive feedback I get when an audience "digs"me. It's exhilarating.

Like anyone in my field (comics and business performers, and other performers in general), once you experience that "high," there's no turning back. Laughter and smiles from the audience are truly addictive. With each experience, you rack up confidence and personal power like hits on a dartboard. Nothing like a bunch of bull's eyes! And once you do score, it's hard to turn back—to do it the old, not-funny way. That's what I've come to know as a hardcore reality. I want you to experience the same joy, for I know that once you do, it will boost your courage to sniff out "times and places" to do your magic. (Nothing like making your audience fall in love with you!)

MAKE SOMEONE HAPPY

What's certainly more important than personal gratification (yours and mine), however, is what I know humor does for the audience. As I mentioned earlier, just about everyone in the business community encounters situations that leave them stressed, overworked, tense, and very much caught up in the business crisis du jour. And I think that helping them take a time-out by providing a little levity—no matter how businesslike the situation may be—is doing them a tremendous service.

I think each of us would agree that making other people feel good—especially providing relief—is a real personal victory. So buy into the idea that it really is your job to provide humor and good stories, each time and place, because entertaining your audience is, in fact, a genuine value. Don't bail. Don't decide at this juncture that although all the lessons in this book make sense, you just don't think you should attempt to put them into play because it might not be the "right time or place." You can build confidence in knowing "when" and "where" much the same way you've honed your delivery and your style. It takes guts and practice. But, as I've urged, you can do it!

TASTES GOOD

Interestingly, most of my students feel relatively confident when it comes to believing they have good taste. Sometimes they're right, and sometimes they're not. Unfortunately, many only find out when they're not!

I've already laid out what is appropriate in terms of broad guidelines, but you have to ask yourself each time you're ready to tell a story or fire off a joke: Is this material in good taste for this particular "given circumstance"?

I'll give you an example. Once I was in a meeting where I was presenting an outline of my "Humor In The Workplace" workshop. There were six principal decision-makers at the conference table. Three were women. One of them looked as though she had been crying, I thought. Her eyes appeared puffy and slightly red. As I began, I noticed she was nervously moving an imaginary ring up and down her barren left "ring" finger. I wasn't sure if she was going through a divorce or had just turned in her engagement ring but my quick observation triggered a red flag about my use of the example I typically share about my own divorce. (I tell a story about how I was so traumatized, I put my triangular underwear on sideways—and how it both startled and cracked me up when I noticed. I also share that, to this day, I purposely wear my underwear that way when times are tough, just as a lighthearted reminder that there is humor in the face of anything.) This tidbit, extracted from my workshop lecture, often entices those who buy my services to want more. I wasn't sure what this gal's situation was, but I wasn't going to take any chances.

Instead, I quickly pulled up another fun personal-experience story from my mental computer screen—a story that would sell them on my work without hurting this woman's feelings or making her feel the slightest bit uncomfortable. To have shared my original story choice would have been in extremely bad taste. So I didn't refer to the high trauma and what absurd things can happen, when going through a horrible breakup, I quickly switched gears to opt for a substitution. (I think I gave the example of how I once threw a surprise birthday party for myself). Again, I'm not certain what her "given circumstance" was, but I did sense that to have shared my planned story would have made everyone in that room cringe. And, incidentally, in case you're wondering: The story about my underwear is told in very good taste so as not to embarrass anyone or to step over that "inappropriate line". I've told it many times with hilarious response from both sexes in an assortment of "given circumstances."

The lesson here is: opt for safety. If you think your story may be objectionable, don't tell it. If you think your joke might be received as "bad taste" from just one person, move on. If you think you may hurt someone's feelings, throw out something that won't offend. Know that another "time," another "place," it just might work—but not "here" and not "now." Don't use any joke or story if you have any question about taste.

Now a few guidelines that will help you establish a way in which to judge what may or may not be good taste:

1. Check out the room and the people in it. Like me, you may have told a certain story a dozen times and had it work, but will it work this time, in this "given circumstance"? Be observant and alert. Look around. Pick up the vibe. Watch for overt and covert signals that let you know the boundaries. What may be in good taste one day may not be on another. Make a judgment call and opt for the "safety zone."

2. When it comes to good taste in general: Ask yourself if what you're about to say would make those who love you the most feel embarrassed. If the answer is "yes," then take a pass. Those close to us typically cut us a great deal of slack in the "taste" department. If what we're about to share would make *them* feel uncomfortable it's a pretty good bet that the people you're standing before aren't going to think much of it, either. Be quick and agile enough to make a substitution.

3. Though there may be times and places in the business world where swearing may be acceptable, don't risk it. It's not worth it. I have found there is always one person who gets offended. You don't ever want someone to tell

someone else that parts of your speech or presentation were not done in good taste, simply because you let go a "dammit," or even a "screw." Keep language above board any "time" and in all "places"—not only to be smart, but also more classy.

4. It's always the right "time and place" to tell stories and throw out humor that compliments the people you're with. An example might be: "Everyone take note of Jon Miller. He could be the poster boy for smiles. He's got a smile bigger than the Astrodome!" This is a fun little aside I once used that fit the "given circumstance." I have found that flattering someone humorously (and sincerely)—whether they're present or not—is always a tasteful way to impart humor or a story.

5. Good taste goes hand in hand with good manners. Dial up all those things your mother taught you, such as "If you can't say anything nice, don't say it at all," "Do unto others…," and "Don't be a smart aleck."

6. It's never in good taste to show disregard. This applies to reckless remarks about the company's bottom line, the meager bonus, or something odd about someone's physical appearance. I can't think of one "time or place" or instance when lack of consideration was a green light in the taste department. There will never be a right time for these jokes and stories. Delete.

7. Sharing a story that is past tense—i.e., how the company you're addressing once floundered—may be acceptable. If, on the other hand, you're projecting that the same company may crash in the future, forget it. It's bad taste to put anyone down. If you want to play with their "past" in a fun and flattering way, that works. We covered that in the previous chapter.

8. Should you make a mistake: Learn to recover quickly. Throw the joke back on you. It's good taste to demonstrate you goofed.

9. The sensitivity factor is a big one. It should always be your focus when considering "right time" and "right place." You can short-cut all other ways of making a

decision on what might—or might not be—in good taste, when you simply stay sensitive to the people you're talking to.

BASIC INSTINCTS

Simply falling back on innate instincts will help steer you in the right direction when it comes to good taste and time and place. Don't forget: you need to tap into that inner voice to determine what's "right time and place."

The following are a few suggestions for developing your instincts:

1. If you're planning a speech or presentation and you craft a joke or story that you count on using, pay attention to the "feeling" you get as you make that selection. Does it "feel" right? Is there some trepidation on your part? Do you "just know" it works for you, but instantly waiver on whether it will work for "them". Listen, listen, listen. Your instincts rarely lead you astray. There is some force in each of us, I believe, that just tends to know what to say "when." If you question this, think about all those times you went with your instincts to say soothing and comforting (and humorous) things to friends and family and business colleagues, just because you felt deeply (on the spur of the moment) it was definitely "the right time and place" to do so.

2. Notice how many times a day you tend to rely on your "instincts." They can be simple things like purposely popping up the toast early because you just sensed it might slightly burn. Or, getting in the "right" line at the bank teller window. You may not have realized how often you rely on your basic instinct for everyday decisions. That being the case, make a log. Keep track. You'll be both surprised and delighted to note how perceptive you really are and how many times an hour (!) you come to rely on your instincts. All this counts big when you start relying on instinct to keep you on track in terms of just "knowing" right time and place in every speech, presentation and even those important one-on-one moments.

3. Since you're taking note, begin to tally how many times your "first impression" of something or someone was right on. We just seem to "know"… I once had a funny (bad) feeling about a guy who stood next to me in an elevator in my office complex. He was later arrested for murder! Yikes.
4. Understand what "instinct" really is. I like to define it as knowing something before you even or ever really rationally know it. Can you see how developing, and paying close attention to, your instincts and intuition will lead you when it comes to "time and place".

Every situation and circumstance will ultimately dictate what is appropriate, so it's nearly impossible to provide you a given formula for knowing "right time and right place". Instead, you need to develop that ear to hear that "inkling" and let the rest take care of itself.

Start out slowly in developing confidence by practicing in low-risk situations. "Right time and place" become automatic after you get confident enough. I know many comics and especially improv players who never worry about "right time and place"; they're very much on auto-pilot. That self-trust keeps them uninhibited, which in turn allows them to take advantage of many an opportunity. Enough practice, and ultimate success, also breeds more of the same. So do the prescribed lessons and get more comfortable in knowing you'll say all the right things at the right time and in the right place.

Now, it's time to learn where and how to go after material you may want to use for your humor and good storytelling, as well as creating original material of your own.

Chapter 9

YOU THINK *THAT'S* FUNNY?: HOW TO CREATE, COMPOSE, AND GATHER HUMOR FOR SPEECHES AND PRESENTATIONS

Now that you've gone to great lengths to master your delivery and determine what's appropriate and what's not (and the right time and right place for your jokes and stories), here comes yet another critical moment. It's time to learn how to either write suitable material or find it.

How to do that? The speechmakers I know come upon their material in several different ways. Some insist on writing their own jokes and stories, while others pay to have people do it for them. Then there are those who buy books full of jokes and humorous tidbits, or search the Internet looking for the same. There are even those who steal their stuff from other speakers or comics!

As with so much else we've covered in this book, there is no one magical way to go about coming up with the material you'll use; in the end, it's simply a matter of preference. That being the case, let's explore the various available options and see which one is right for you. We'll begin at the beginning. You need to define a few foundational elements before you write or seek out your jokes and stories.

READY, SET, CREATE

The following assignments will help you define your direction in terms of content; they will get you going on the right track. Incidentally, these steps can be repeated before assembling material for any and all of your speeches and presentations—from those that last five minutes to the ones that extend all the way through an eight-hour workshop. Here we go:

1. Take a look at your speech or presentation and assess how many jokes and/or stories you think you'll need and/or want to include in order to spice up your performance. If you're not sure, let me make a couple of recommendations. I think you always need an icebreaker; that's a given. I also suggest you let no more than a few minutes go by without some kind of humor or interesting story. One way to find a strategic juncture at which to interject such items is to do an appraisal of your overall content. Pinpoint exactly where you will complete various passages of information, ideas, or important points. If your speech is written out, make a pen or pencil mark at these definitive junctures. If your speech is in outline form, insert bullet points with asterisks at the appropriate moments. These marks will serve as "flags."

    Now, as you continue on with this assignment, decide that you will cap off each of these transitional moments with either a joke or an interesting story. I'll provide an example: I was once discoursing on the fears of public speaking and how we all seem to share a common sense of fright about getting "up there" all by ourselves. During one section of the speech, I ran down a menu of physical and mental ills we go through—from cotton mouth to simply wanting one thing: your mother—when there we are and it's suddenly "time" (!) I finished off this crucial section of my speech with a one-liner I just love from Lily

Tomlin. It goes: "Don't forget: we're all in this alone!" Then I continued on, inserting one more one-liner or story to similarly close off each subsequent message.

2. Next, decide the nature of the "given audience" and check out the "given circumstance." These, of course, will have to be factors currently known to you; I'm not referring now to your more spontaneous material because what we're addressing here is your writing and gathering material ahead of time. Dealing with the "givens" will help you as you decide what stories and jokes are appropriate to tell. This task requires you to carefully tally up some specifics. Your choices for light moments during a eulogy, quite obviously, will differ greatly from those you choose for a free-for-all roast. So stand back and make a reasonable assessment of the "situation." This will provide you with guidelines for the following assignment.

3. Make a list of topics you could cover—tossing in a joke here and a story there—that you know would be in good taste and match the event. In other words, whatever it is you're talking about should be enhanced or complemented by a bit of humor that relates.

Example: I once spoke to a group of female executives, all of whom, I was told, were raising families while simultaneously trying to make the "big time." I was to share with them my own career trials and how I advanced myself, despite the obstacles. I made a list of topics I thought they would relate to and find fun, if not hilarious. Many of them were my own personal experiences. I jotted down: men, end of workday, cooking dinner, etc. Next to each of these ideas I wrote a corresponding thought. Men—differences in the way men and women get off to work in the a.m. (they shave, we make-up like every day's the Prom). Cooking dinner—fast food, junk food, and no food, or hell, I'll just have a bag of Lay's. End of workday—the joy of laundry, guess who gets to run back out for milk, and "Not tonight—it's not the headache—I'm exhausted and out of chocolate!"

After I've compiled a list of thoughts—created suitable ideas—for the crowd I'm going to encounter, then I can either script a few one-liners, find quotes from others on the subject, or dredge up some real hard-hitting stories that coincide. And that's how I suggest you go about this "getting started" process—that is, getting your humor and stories on track.

4. Remember: The high commandment of the *"What's So Funny?"* rulebook is that *every* single speech or presentation is deserving of humor and good stories. No copping out, then, by deciding that because you're talking about last quarter's earnings, there is no opportunity for levity. There is, in every speech, if you allow it. I repeat: We can be funny not just sometimes—but every time we present or perform before others. Humor is needed and appreciated all the way around. So set your mind in that groove.

Doing the above assignments is the best and most practical way to initially "create" the type of material you'll use. The ideas you'll generate through the assignments will guide and direct you, whether you end up writing your joke and storytelling content yourself, or look elsewhere for it.

I often look within, at my "innermost thoughts and feelings" (I talked about this earlier, if you recall), for things that will summon appropriate subject matter and tidbits. Such introspection serves beautifully as the foundation for all my original writing of colorful content—or as a compass to guide me to where I can find it. Once gathered, such ideas and scraps of information can be fleshed out in many different ways, i.e., one-liners, quick jokes, witty words of wisdom, or stories with flair. So I take what I get and use it wisely.

Here's another way to come by the "beginnings" of your humorous content and stories. I'll tell you what I tell my sketch-writing students: "Pick a theme or point" before you write anything. This forces you to grab hold of what it is you *want* to share (i.e., what makes you angry, fearful, frustrated, happy, etc.). The next logical step is the act of seeking out specific jokes and stories that will go with such themes and points, and of course, related feelings about them. A prime and recent example: When I spoke to the women's group I referred to, I wanted to make the point that women simply have far more demands than men when it comes to career and the management of a family. Women tend to take on more responsibility than men. So I chose ideas that catered to that precise point, and I expressed my utter frustration about the whole thing all through my light "flag" moments.

Once you have your ideas together, it's time to choose one of the four options for getting to the finish line: Writing your own material, paying someone else to write it, discovering it in books, or "lifting" it from someone else.

THE WRITE STUFF

Your first choice is write your own material—make up your own stuff. It's not nearly as tough as you might think. If you have your thoughts collected on the points you wish to make, then you can start the process quite easily.

If it's a joke you're after, decide whether it's a one-liner or a short tidbit with a punchline. Then make another decision: Are you going to invent the joke, or speak from a real-life frame of reference? If you're going to make it up—fabricate it—which is not the least bit harmful—then decide what I tell my sketch writers to decide: "what's the point?" Once you know your objective, it's easy to come upon a one-liner or a punchline.

Example: I often talk about the importance of money and theories behind how we all spend it. I wanted to throw in a humorous one-liner in front a group of financial planners (who, I knew, were far more conservative than I). I began to explain how I had grown up with parents who behaved like they were *still* living in the Depression and how they were always saving, saving, saving. As a child, it created a mind-set of "lack"—which made me rebelliously reckless with money as a young adult. Forget saving—I told the financial planners—"My philosophy is: If you can't eat it or wear it, don't buy it!"

I wrote the line myself, which elicited a big laugh, by the way. And it was originated out of a mere frame of reference. I'm certain you, too, have humorous thoughts that jet through your mind from time to time—ideas, based upon your perspective of the world and your own personal experiences in it. As they come to you, write these thoughts down. I have a whole database of one-liners. I call them up at appropriate moments. They include philosophies about the things in life that strike a nerve in me, make me happy, mad, etc. They are all based upon my own observations, opinions, and points of view.

I'll bet you hadn't thought about jotting such thoughts and ideas down before, and moreover, hadn't thought that they would become fodder for comedy material. What's more, you probably never thought you would become a "comedy writer" by simply recording those fleeting thoughts. I very often come upon ExecuProv students who swear there is no way they can write their own material, but I soon convince them otherwise. It's not nearly as hard as they think, I tell them. I ask them, and now I'm asking you, to return to Chapter Two in this book. Part of your assignment in that chapter was to explore the work of comics. If you take a second glance at their routines, you'll see that many of their "cracks" were nothing more than their own philosophies. They saved them as they came into their minds—then wrote them down, knowing they would one day use them as one-liners.

One-liners can be similes, metaphors, analogies, maxims, and your original sayings or cliches. The exercise you just did to come up with them can also be utilized as you compose punchlines to jokes. In other words, you may have a "point" in mind, but, perhaps you need a little explanation—build— before you hit that punchline. If you go back to your "innermost thoughts and feelings" and write them out (maybe edit them once or twice for clarity), then add a "finish"—you have your joke. Amazing! And to think, you wrote it yourself! That's all there is to it.

Just keep track of those zingers that tend to spring up— the ones that make you smile or throw back your head with a deep chuckle as you pensively take a shower, drive the freeway, cook dinner, brush the dog—for they are all great sources of original material.

My dear friend Michael Gellman, who works at Second City in Chicago and is one of the most revered improvisational comedy directors in the field, says "writing is rewriting." Know, then, that you may have to whip out several drafts before your written joke or story works. Few of us comedy writers get the final product the first time out. We, too, keep "working the piece" until it gels. That could take several drafts.

One more selling point about writing your own material: Nothing is more pleasing to any audience than original material. Since each of us is so different, it's fascinating to every audience to get "our take" on things. So, even if you've never written anything, give writing your humor and stories a try. I think you'll be pleasantly surprised. Too, you never run the risk of people's having already heard "that joke."

Even if you ultimately decide to choose one of the other options as a method by which to come upon your material, give this first option a valiant effort. It's great for stretching those mental muscles, and it will give you such a great sense of pride and accomplishment!

COMEDY FOR SALE

If you find that writing your own material is just not your forte, or you don't have time to search and explore and keep a database, then you can always hire one or more people to write humor and stories for you. Most people are shocked to learn how easy it is to go this route. Lots of my corporate executives think it might be too costly to hire someone to write their stuff, but if you know where and how to shop, that's not the case.

The only trick is getting very clear on what it is you're looking for. Knowing what kind of jokes will complement your dialogue is important.

But let's say, for the sake of argument, that you just don't know. That's okay, too. You can take your script or your outline to the right writer, and that person will help you define those specifics. After all, that's part of their job.

First, let's talk about finding "that" writer. There are several ways to go about it:

1. Contact local comedy clubs, comedy schools, or comedy theaters to ask if they have students, actors, or teachers who are not only comedic actors and directors, but writers, as well. When you contact these potential

writers, ask for references. Also ask for samples of their work, even if the samples are not speeches, per se; it will give you a strong indication of their style and whether their "voice" would be harmonious with your speechwriting/humor needs.

During your first meeting or telephone conversation with a prospect, let them know specifically what you need: someone to write jokes and stories for your speech or presentation, of course, but also your boundaries and what would be comfortable for you. Next, query them on how they would go about servicing your writing needs. They may present a concept or concepts initially, then after you approve them, they may offer a draft (even one-liners go through this process). I always suggest you ask that they send a few concepts based on your specifications, before they launch into a finished product. In the end, as the two of you pass drafts back and forth, you may find that you're becoming a bona fide comedy writer! It's a great way to break in and gain confidence for when you decide to give writing a whirl on your own.

Four of the best improv centers in the country are Second City (in Chicago), The L.A. Groundlings (in Los Angeles), Capital Steps (in Washington, D.C.), and The Orange County Crazies (in Santa Ana, CA). In your part of the country, look up improv comedy schools and groups. Make certain they have a good and long-standing reputation. Once you determine that they do, tap into them. Chances are their resources are bountiful. Budding and starving comics collect at such places. Many are trying to earn a living, in addition to getting a career off the ground. They will not only be delighted to hear from you, they probably are quite reasonable in terms of pricing.

2. If that search doesn't pan out, call any of the network television stations and ask for the production offices of any sitcom. Next, ask them for agents or PR representatives of the writers on their show. These representatives have lots of budding writers on their rosters who may be willing to work on the side to make a living. Something

else you should be aware of is that many of their clients are "in between" jobs, and they need income. You would be surprised at how many sources you'll come upon by contacting these people.
3. Contact the theater departments at universities and colleges known for their excellence in theater and film. They include Northwestern University in Chicago, UCLA in Los Angeles, Chapman College in Orange, California, and Harvard (*Saturday Night Live* gets many of its writers from the *Harvard Lampoon* staff).
4. Lastly, contact conservatories such as Juilliard or Carnegie Mellon and see what leads they can provide. You can also go on the Internet and look under college or conservatory theater departments and query them.

While I think the first few suggestions—going after aspiring comics in comedic-oriented venues—are the best ones, the others are worthy of exploration as well. But before you pick up the phone, also consider the following options:
1. Run an ad in one of the theater publications, such as *Backstage West/Dramalogue*—or even the *Hollywood Reporter* or *Daily Variety*. Actors read these publications to learn about what auditions are being held, but writers and directors do, too. These publications are famous for keeping the "aspiring" types apprised of opportunities in their field). Each publication has a classified section that will run a small ad such as yours (i.e., corporate exec needs comedy writer to aid in speechwriting). Each region of the country has its own such publications; however, research the bigger cities and especially New York, L.A., and Chicago for the best sources. Those are the towns these people migrate to in order to launch careers.
2. Post a notice at theatrical bookstores such as Applause in New York, Samuel French in Los Angeles or Act Two in Chicago. You can send a flier to the store (with your ad) and they just may post it. Lots of good writers hang out at these stores. Remember, your goal here is to tap into unknown but skilled comedy writers who could really dress up your speech and presentation.

3. Search the Internet. Many comedy organizations and clubs have web sites. Those with direct links can easily prove a valuable resource.
4. Next, you can call companies such as mine—ExecuProv—that specialize in speech coaching and writing and can provide writing services. I spend about one fourth of my professional time providing themes and writing material for many of my Fortune 500 clients.
5. Ask fellow speechmakers (who you think are really funny) who they use. Maybe they have someone ghostwriting their material. You never know.
6. Contact video production companies (who work for corporations and companies to prepare trade shows, product video shoots and meetings and conventions) and ask them for references. Often these companies use a pool of writers, many of whom are very familiar with what flies and what doesn't when it comes to comedy in corporate America.

There is simply no excuse for not finding a suitable writer who can help you with your humor and storytelling—because they are everywhere! So if you don't want to write your own stuff, get resourceful. Ask around. Check out all of the above sources.

BOOK WORMING

Another method you can employ to get the "write stuff" is to start your own library. Borders, Barnes and Noble, and Amazon.com have hundreds of titles that offer up a slew of jokes, humorous quotes, and witty stories. The following is just a partial list of books I have on hand:

*__1001 More Great Jokes__ by Jess Rovin
*__1001 More Humorous Illustrations for Public Speaking__ by Michael Hodgin
*__101 Wacky Computer Jokes__ by Genevieve Stamper
*__The 2,548 Best Things Anybody Ever Said__ by Robert Byrne

*****2000 Sure Fire Jokes for Speakers and Writers: The Encyclopedia of One-Liner Comedy** by Robert Orben
*****2100 Laughs for All Occasions** by Robert Orben
*****2400 Jokes to Brighten Your Speeches** by Robert Orben
*****250 Funniest Office Jokes, Memos & Cartoon Pinups** by Adam Warlock
*****2500 Jokes to Start 'Em Laughing** by Robert Orben
*****3500 Good Jokes for Speakers** by Jerry Leiberman and Gerald F. Lieberman
*****A-Z Sparkling Illustrations: Stories, Anecdotes and Humor for Speakers** by Stephen Gaukorger and Nick Mercer (contributor)
*****Instant Quotation Dictionary** by Donald Bolander
*****Best Quotations for All Occasions** by Lewis Henry
*****Peter's Quotations: Ideas for Our Time** by Laurence Peter
*****Quoteunquote: The Game of Humorous and Revealing Quotes** by Paul R. Winslow
*****Humorous Quotations** by Des MacHale and Sean MacHale

There are, obviously, dozens of others, so do some scouting around. Perhaps you can't afford to furnish an entire library initially, but you can do what I've done over the years. I just add a new book to my shelves every couple of months.

Another suggestion is that you peruse the comedy and public-speaking sections of the bookstores I've mentioned as well as those in your hometown. There, too, you will find some real jewels. Jerry Seinfeld, Paul Reiser, Bill Cosby, and Tim Allen—all of whom have written books—may have some wonderful anecdotes you can use (and properly attribute, please).

In sum, if you don't want to write your own material, just know there is a cornucopia of sources available in libraries, and bookstores, and on the Internet.

By the way, I tell all my students who choose to write their own material that they should still build a hefty library of such books. They just may stimulate ideas or simply serve as inspiration.

One last book I want to mention is Judy Carter's **Stand-Up Comedy, The Book**, (Dell Publishing). Ms. Carter is the most highly revered stand-up comedy teacher in the country, and an absolute genius when it comes to helping people come into their talent. Her book is a must-have!

BEG, BORROW BUT STEAL?

This last option is my least favorite. It's the "lift" choice—that is, stealing someone else's proven material and using it as your own. For the record, although I know many people who do this, I don't recommend it—for many reasons.

First of all, it's just bad manners! I feel strongly that it's morally wrong to lift someone's original material and call it your own. It's one thing if you choose to credit them—although you should still get their permission; but to use someone's joke or story and pretend it's new is in bad taste. Period.

I once sat in the audience, unbeknownst, and listened to a speaker, who had the audacity to lift one of my personal stories! It was a bit I often share about how tough times were for me and my sister when we were both single mothers. It goes: One year, my sister had only enough money for a Christmas tree, but nothing extra to buy trimmings for it. (She'd lost the ones she'd accumulated during her last move.) She was extremely depressed. When she left to go to the store, I enlisted my two oldest children and my parents and suggested we get really clever and decorate the tree with various odds and ends from around the house. We scurried, because we had only about 20 minutes before my sister was due to return. We draped the tree with shreds of stapled napkins (to give it a flocked effect), ripped tabs from Pampers (my niece was there with her baby), Q-tips, and paper clips. We used tightly rolled maxi-pads to create "snowball bulbs." Twinkie cellophane wrappers created some glitter. Then we crowned it with a Jolly Green Giant Bean can (where the angel would normally go). We also added a few other random elements at the last minute—empty cigarette packs and marshmallows. Believe it or not, it was not only hilarious to look at (and the talk of the condo complex), but also one of the prettiest and most sentimental trees I've ever decorated. But getting back to my point: This speaker was suddenly telling my story—with the exact same details—as though it was her own. I nearly jumped from the gallery and screamed "Treason! That was my tree, dammit!" but decided to wait. As she was being congratulated by attendees at the conclusion of her speech, I slowly walked by. She caught my eye. I glared as she gasped and turned Christmas-bulb red! I turned and just kept walking. I later learned she got drunk in the bar and loudly confessed that she was a thief. I'm sure she now thinks of me not only every time she considers using someone else's story, but also whenever she decorates a Christmas tree.

The lesson here is that none of us wants bad speechmaking karma. And that old saying about "what goes around comes around" can rear its truthful head if ever someone you didn't expect shows up for your speech. Even if I hadn't been there, a friend in attendance who remembered my story may have reported the incident back to me. And what about the person in the audience who doesn't know me but who sat in on a speech where I told that story? So much for respect for the speaker who stole it! It's not worth taking such chances.

Sadly, this speaker could have gotten the same comedic value out of my story while keeping her integrity intact—if she'd only attributed the story to me. She could have prefaced it by saying, "This gal I once heard speak told the funniest story...I just have to pass it on..." But NOOOOO (as John Belushi used to say)...and she got caught! Not a good thing—this kind of embarrassment—for anyone, especially the business professional. It's always a small world.

Morality notwithstanding, you can also get sued. And stealing someone else's material—intellectual property, whether it's Steve Martin's or the speaker-next-door's—is not legal. Plagiarism can be both a state and federal offense, and the fines can be hefty. Besides, who wants to endure a lengthy and costly lawsuit for the price of a few laughs? My advice: If you love a joke or story so much, always credit the author. If you can get their permission in writing, all the better. If not, at least set up your jokes and stories with verbal footnotes that acknowledge the source. Not only will others continue to respect you, you will also feel better about yourself. Every performer should have a great sense of "self"!

What I often suggest to my students is to watch other comics and speakers and learn from their jokes and stories what might stimulate ideas that they may have in their own repertory. Ideas that are similar but not exact. For example, the grinch who stole my Christmas tree story could have searched her mental bank for a similar situation and then shared her own story of how she managed a tough time as a single mom. (She let us know she was one.) Using her own personal experience could have been just as fun and pleasing to the audience. So, don't steal other people's material; instead, see what their material triggers in your mind that might remind you of a funny experience in your life—one you can share with honesty and pride. There is something to be said for authenticity. Somehow we just know when someone's material is not their own.

PICK AND CHOOSE

As you can see, there are many ways in which you can create, compose and gather your own material to spice up your speeches and presentations. Perhaps one of the four options will be the constant choice for you, but then again, you may end up using each of the four at different times for different reasons.

What I want you to understand is that you have all the resources needed (and more!) to write or access humor and stories, time after time after time! And, in closing, I want to suggest that you use as much creativity as you can muster when designing your jokes and stories. Don't use the same jokes and stories continually. They'll probably get stale. Challenge yourself to come up with new and dazzling material. I would recommend at least one new joke or story for every time you give that same speech or teach that same class or workshop.

If you're constantly testing yourself, you'll gain a great sense of confidence. My improv players love doing improv for that very reason. What they do is never, ever the same. They can be assigned the same formatted piece (like a traditional game-show premise we do from time to time), but because all the input from the audience is entirely different from show to show, the piece will always be fresh and funny!

Think like an improv player now and stretch those mental muscles. For, even though you have conquered your delivery, your material is equally important. The pros are always finding something extra—something different or unusual—to add to their material and performances to keep them on their toes.

My biggest reason for wanting you to go about this with such energy is that, over time, it builds a tremendous amount of discipline and confidence. It also means that people will always look forward to sitting in on your speeches and presentations—because they know they'll be delightfully surprised each time they do. There is so much to be said for unpredictability when it comes to entertainment! And, if you're a speaker or presenter, you are, indeed, an entertainer.

Chapter 10

NOT THAT FUNNY: JUST GOOD STORYTELLING

Maybe you're the kind of speaker and presenter who shies away from humor and instead leans toward telling interesting stories in order to spice up your speeches or presentations. If so, good for you. Your ability to tell a good story can be just as entertaining as humor—just ask any audience. I feel strongly that humor is not the only way in which to liven up a performance. Storytelling, if done well, can be just as pleasing.

I love a good story. I think we all do. And captivating storytelling isn't nearly as difficult to master as joke-telling; it's something most of us do every day. Storytelling is simply the act of recounting an event or situation for someone who wasn't there when it happened. In my opinion, if we're not already, we should all learn to be good storytellers because it is the ability to share a story that makes us stand out from all the rest of the crowd—those other humdrum speakers and presenters.

Every speech or presentation should be peppered with stories. Some of my favorite speeches have been the ones that were presented with the use of one story after another to convey the overall messages. No one can tune out a good story!

But (I can hear you asking): What constitutes a good story, and what constitutes good *storytelling*? My mission in this chapter is to answer these two important questions.

If you recall, we've already addressed storytelling to some degree in earlier chapters. I talked about the origin of our interest in hearing a good story: It began when listening to our parents either tell us or read us one. Also, in earlier chapters, I discussed how sharing your innermost thoughts and feelings invites your audiences "inside your head," and how doing so is the very basis or key to learning to tell a captivating story. Midway through the book, as I focused on delivery, I also discussed "build," "momentum," and "beats." I even asked you to stand in front of the mirror or before a trusted friend or family member and recount an event in your own words.

So, in effect you already know something about some of the mechanics of storytelling; however, the assignments I have prescribed thus far emphasized putting a humorous spin on your story and making sure your delivery followed through on the promise.

Now it's time to put the humor aspect aside for a moment and simply concentrate on good old-fashioned storytelling—storytelling for storytelling's sake. *Any* story can be funny, but I like speakers who can mix it up—who have the versatility to offer up both hilarious and poignant moments. I'm sure you feel as I do. It can often be the more serious moments—those touching "side bars"—that stick with me. As a speaker, I like to surprise my audience with at least one serious story in any speech or presentation, just for a change of pace. Contrast and variety make us interesting. And balance, in terms of content, is very effective in any presentation. Too much humor, and sometimes the audience won't take us seriously. Those occasional hard-hitting stories can pack quite a punch.

JUST GOOD THEATER

If you think about it, "straight" stories are just good theater. And even in the most outrageous comedies, I think everyone enjoys an intriguing or heartfelt moment or two. One of my all-time favorite "stories" is the film *Planes, Trains and Automobiles,* with John Candy and Steve Martin. Much of the movie is very funny, yet there are certain moments that serve up an appropriate measure of pathos. For instance, when

Candy, the shower-curtain-ring salesman, boldly states that he didn't care for the manner in which Martin blasted him—about his leaving the bathroom a mess, and hogging the blankets, and what a loser he was in the motel where they shared the same bed—it was done with such a mixture of sentiment that I had a hard time not crying. It really touched me. So did the scene in the train station when Candy finally confessed to Martin he had no wife.

Good stories, I think, are a product of good "theater" in any form—on stage or on the screen—and can be just as indelible. And, again, they don't have to be the least bit funny. If you'll notice, even the funniest comedy will have a serious moment or two (Woody Allen movies are rife with them); at the same time, the most serious films can also have times of humor. *Terms of Endearment* and *Forrest Gump* are two of my favorites. How about you?

Your first assignment, then, is to list a few of your favorite all-time movies—the ones that had a "great story," in your estimation. Next, I'd like to ask that you take in a few movies; either comedies or dramas, and notice when the comedies inject some seriousness and when the dramas engage in a light moment or two. The point of this assignment is for you to see how effective the contrast is when both humor and drama are present and how both elements are the backbone of what makes a story a story. Also, how humor and pathos can go hand in hand to weave the details of most stories. This two-part assignment is a prerequisite in order for you to understand the "telling" of a good story. Until you can recognize what makes a good story good, it will be hard for you to create and tell your own.

As in other assignments, be sure to take notes. They will be most helpful as you sit quietly to compose special storytelling moments in your upcoming speeches and stories. And remember: Good stories are synonymous with good theater. In the end, that's all a story is: a good "show".

BEGINNING, MIDDLE, AND END

As you go about analyzing films, I also want you to take note the parts of a story and examine what holds a story together. Having been a writer for many years, and a teacher, I believe a good story must always include a beginning, a middle, and an end. When I teach my writing or scene-study improv classes, this three-part concept is one of the first things I acquaint my students with. Understanding this, and understanding how to delineate one juncture from the next, serves as the basis for all meaningful storytelling work.

As I tell my students, the beginning situates the audience. In other words, it provides a who, what, why, where, and when. And in providing such information, it sets up for the audience what we term a "stage picture"—just like what we would immediately see as we flip from one television channel to the next. We get a visual.

Here's an example (pretend you're the audience as I begin this story): " It was just before Christmas and I was helping to take care of my mother, who was suffering from cancer. She was extremely ill. We were in her family room, and we were talking, and suddenly, as she lay on her favorite sofa, she dropped her glass of water. Spilled it all over her lap and side and…" As you can see, I have clearly situated you, the audience—set you up, as it were—to "take you there"—to give you a picture of what, who, etc. By my doing so, you were able to settle into my story as well as reasonably anticipate whatever I might share next.

So, as you go about constructing or improvising your stories, always remember, to "situate" your audience first. It acclimates them as well as sets them up for what's coming next. Nothing more intriguing than anticipation.

Quite obviously, what comes next is the middle: The point where you begin to get to the conflict, the issue, the "point" of the story. To illustrate, I'll continue with the middle segment of the story I was telling about my ailing mother. "…I just began to freak out. She was laying there drenched with water. It was nearly impossible to change her clothes, let alone move her to a drier spot. She wasn't real heavy, but just too heavy for me alone to pick her up. So I began blurting every soothing thing I could think of, like 'It's okay, Mom,' 'I'll clean it up. Don't worry,' and so on. Meantime, she's struggling to lift herself off the sofa to drier land..." As you can see, I'm getting to the crux of the story. I continue: " 'No. Mom. Don't get up. Please. Just let me... ' She started to cry, and I felt so helpless. Then I had a brainstorm. I think things like that happen in a crisis. Not just for me but for all of us. I raced down the hall toward her bedroom, yelling over my shoulder all the way. My voice was trailing behind me and getting louder as I ran. I said, 'Don't get up Mom, I'll be right back.' I tore through her bathroom cupboard like I was on some time-ticking game show until I reached her hair dryer. I ripped it out of that cupboard so fast, Q-tips and cotton balls and lipsticks were flying every which way. I didn't care. I was terrified she'd try to get up, and I knew she couldn't walk. She'd fall. I bolted through the door and began running in her direction, hairdryer in hand..."

So, there's my middle. And with this middle, you get a very clear picture of what, sequentially, followed the beginning. If all of this seems incredibly obvious to you—hey, I know people who start their story at the end or the middle and forget the beginning altogether. Conversely, I know people who tell the middle and beginning, only to trail off leaving the ending to our imaginations. So, as basic as all this may seem, I want you to carefully examine the most recent story you shared and ask yourself if it started with a reasonable beginning and subsequently traveled along to a sequential middle?

Now, getting back to my story. It's time to bring it to resolution—provide closure for you, the audience. Here goes: "...and then I ran frantically down the hall. As I came into view, my mother looked at me and could barely mumble: 'What the hell are you doing?' I said, 'Don't move, Mom.' I plugged in the hair dryer and blew her dry! It took a few minutes, but it worked. No need to change her clothes—to worry about how I would lift her. No need to panic further. The warmth of the blower was soothing to her—and actually, to me, too. Under my breath I thanked God that there was at least *one* small thing I could do to make her feel better! Ah, all was well until the next desperate moment. And there were a number of them as

I cared for my mother. The hardest thing I've ever had to do, by the way... I loved her so, so much!"

As you can see, I have just told you a complete story. Although sad, hopefully it was one that kept you interested until the very end as you wondered what finish I might give to it. And, notice: It wasn't a lengthy story—just a tidbit—but an entire story nonetheless.

To recap, then: Good stories are simply a function of sharing good "theater," and each presentation must have a beginning, middle, and end.

CONSTRUCTING AND COMPOSING

Now that you have the basic basics, it's time to move on to the nuts and bolts of crafting stories.

When I teach my sketch writing classes, I talk to my students about an eight-part formula. I'll share three parts of that formula with you quickly now, as I think they will help substantially as you go about the task of creating and writing your own stories—or better yet, simply improvising them whenever and wherever you choose to.

First off, I tell my students to create pieces—sketches—short little stories—that reflect their points of view or their frame of reference. I ask them to jot down their feelings, fears, wants, etc. Next I ask them to come up with a concept to wrap their story (sketch) around. After they pick a concept, they then lay out pivotal points, things or events that move the story from one important moment to the next. These are what we call "beat points." "Beats," in this instance (unlike the earlier ones I discussed that have to do with pauses and timing), help you format an outline of sorts. Each bullet point in this "outline" is expounded on improvisationally (as my students fill in the in-between parts), leading the story from one "beat point" to the next.

As an example, in the story about my mother, my concept centered around the tragedy of caring for a gravely ill parent. My "beat points" included the following junctures: the spilling of the water; my reaction to it; my springing into action to fix the problem, finding a solution and going for it, and my final beat point—blowing her dry.

As you go about laying out your stories before that big speech or presentation, you can always make certain that your stories are complete—that they do in fact have a beginning, middle, and end—by scribbling down your "beat points." My writing students tell me this part of the writing formula is a godsend. You, too can use it—just fill in each "beat point" with appropriate dialogue, and you'll be assured of good, sound stories that stimulate interest and captivate your audiences. Your stories will have a flow to them—an easy-to-assimilate sequence—and will help you stay on track as you "build" them and move them along.

HOW YOU TELL A STORY

How you *tell* a story is as important as how you construct one, so in addition to thinking about the beginning, middle, end, and "beat points," you must also think about your treatment in expressing the particulars of your story in order to bring it to life.

I've talked several times about sharing your innermost thoughts and feelings. And when it comes to telling stories, that's always effective. "Telling it like it is"—taking us there and reliving "it" is also extremely effective. It's what I attempted to do in the story I just shared about my mother. Though you couldn't actually hear my voice as I told it, I will mention that when I did share that story, and got to the part where I tore down the hallway to retrieve my mother's hair dryer, I got louder and more animated and faster-paced in order to convey my sheer panic. I wanted my audience to feel what I was feeling; wanted them to experience it with me. So, whatever story you're telling, always remember we truly want to share it with you—become a part of it—step inside your shoes and live it, too.

For that to happen, you have to have meaning behind your words—you must express yourself—which we also talked about earlier. You have to put forth some emotion and attitude, whatever the tone of your story, in order to sell us, the audience. So, after you've given thought to the creation and construction of each of your stories, also give thought to your performance—to how you will express yourself through the delivery of the story. Think of an actor who has a script in front of him; the script may be very exciting on paper, but how the actor delivers and intones the words will make all the difference in the world as to whether or not the story will execute. In other words, move us as an audience.

Though you did a similar assignment in an earlier chapter, now take a serious or "non-funny" story and "work it." Ask yourself: What attitude is appropriate? How many moods can you utilize to really evoke a response from your audience as you go along (from "beat point" to "beat point")? Every good story has a momentum all its own; we also covered that earlier. But now, I'm asking that you create momentum for a story that doesn't rely on humor—for a story that's just darned interesting or touching.

The very same principals we covered in Chapter Four also apply here. So don't forget, you still need energy, self-expression, spontaneity, timing, and attitude to put your stories across.

For another homework assignment, watch Hal Holbrook doing Mark Twain. Note the content of his stories as well as the manner in which he delivers them. They are not necessarily Pulitzer Prize winning stories, but, ah, the way in which he tells them! Nuances in facial animation, guttural sounds here and there, a whine, even a yelp. I don't care what story he tells, he does it with such style and flair. (That's not to say that every story you tell should be done overly dramatically or out of character for who you are. Play to your strengths. Utilize all the many aspects of *your* talent! It will have such a profound effect on how your well-crafted stories come across.)

After the Holbrook assignment, make a list of other great storytellers you would like to study. These could include guests on Letterman or Leno, preachers, politicians, people who host shows on the History Channel. It could also include people around you—perhaps speechmakers you encounter who really know how to tell a good story. Don't forget what I said earlier: A great actor is a great observer. I always tell my students to study people whose skills are much better than theirs (at that present moment). It has a way of stepping up one's performance level. Many improv players will tell you that, though it's scary at first, they would much rather play on stage with improv artists better than they are, since doing so forces them to rise to greater heights. You too, want to begin to study and hang out with storytellers you regard as "better." See what you can learn from them.

NAILING YOUR STORIES

After you've completed the above assignments, you need to practice putting them together in terms of content. No better way to do that than to take your "beats" and begin crafting them on paper. I suggest you write them out at first, because it really helps bring clarity to each juncture of your story; it also crystallizes where the beginning ends, the middle begins, and where the ending should be. I want to caution you, though, as you go about this assignment: Often the manner in which we write is quite different from the way we talk. Remember that all your stories should be told conversationally—with a natural flow and with a total and utter human touch. If you write your story out, write it as though you're "talking" it. Use words and phrases you would say when talking to your best friend. If you write your stories out and you're not thinking along these lines, your stories may sound stilted and formal. That's the last thing you want! So write the same way you speak.

Next, you can stand in front of the mirror, or just sit quietly, and read your written stories out loud to yourself. Suddenly, you'll get a feel for where the emphasis should go—the pauses—the softer and more dramatic inflections in your voice.

But getting back to writing, it genuinely is a wonderful way to get your skill level up. It really does help you get proficient at sculpting stories that build anticipation as they cover all the pertinent details your audience should hear. In time, because you've studied in this fashion, it can't help but make you a better storyteller.

The other benefit of writing out your stories is that you get to go back over them and revamp them, beef up certain sections, and, overall, give more depth and meaning to the points you want your stories to make.

As a side note, I want to share some behind-the-scenes information as to why stage performers benefit from mastering writing skills, though they never intend to write for a living. I recall Tracy Newman, a former fellow L.A. Groundling and friend (who went on to write for and direct many sitcoms—*The Drew Carey Show*—and produce the hit ABC series *Ellen* with Ellen DeGeneres), telling a reporter once that her mission as a teacher at the Groundlings was not only to prepare her students to perform comfortably and confidently in front of others, but to teach them how to write—never mind that they may have had no interest in following such a career path. "Much by accident," she said, "almost anyone who studied long enough at the Groundlings became a terrific writer."

In fact, many shows (including *Cheers, The Cosby Show, Golden Girls, Just Shoot Me, Third Rock*) have had at the writing helm former L.A. Groundlings who once thought they were going to become performers and nothing more. They were able to capitalize on a wide spectrum of opportunities in the business because they had mastered some pretty important skills. (As you probably know, not all actors get to become actors but opt for other equally rewarding jobs in the industry—writing being among the best of them.) Indirectly, these students and performers were forced to learn to conceptualize and write their sketch material in order to compete for "stage time."

In teaching my students at the Orange County Crazies, I, too, impose certain writing assignments on them as part of their curriculum—even if they wish only to perform improvisational comedy. Such study nurtures the best in terms of their thought processes when they're improvising. They begin to communicate in a more succinct, logical, and meaningful way. And that's what I want for you, too.

For practice, you can also pick up stories written by an author other than yourself—stories you admire—and begin to break down their work. By this, I mean analyze why their stories are so entertaining and complete. You can also take stories and critique them, like a teacher, noting where you think changes could be made to make the story even better.

One last thing—my final comment on this topic—an important reminder: make certain the style in which you write reflects an easy, conversational tone. Your stories shouldn't read like business letters.

OH WHERE, OH WHERE DO THESE STORIES GO?

Let's assume that you've gotten a good grasp of how to put stories together—how to craft them, and how to deliver them with "kick." Now you have to decide exactly where in your speeches and presentations you can put them to good use. Should you use several serious stories in a row? Should you open with a dramatic story? End with one? Use only one "heavy" story so as not to bring the audience down? Are there times to forego stories altogether? Can stories be too long?

Again, you want to review your "given audience" and "given circumstances" in order to make a reasonable assessment and answer each of these questions adequately. As a rule of thumb, however, theory is that you offer enough stories to make your speech or presentation entertaining.

Although it is hard to give you a hard and fast formula, I want you to think about balance. Have you spent four or five minutes on dry, informational material? Have you pounded your audience with hard-hitting persuasive facts only, in order to get them to go your way? Don't go too long or too far without a story. Remember: It's the stories—not the facts—that really sell what you're saying. Too many boring details, and any audience will tune you out. So take a good look at that speech and presentation and try to determine at what points you've gone on too long with the lackluster material. If you're starting to get bored along the way, so will your audience. Remember: Strive for balance. If your material is starting to drag, punch it up with a story.

How about several stories in a row? I think this is a really clever way to teach and persuade. When I teach classes that help students learn how to go about pursuing their acting careers after they've mastered the mechanics, I tell them story after story to make my points—stories that carefully illustrate the information I think they need. So yes, I think in appropriate circumstances, you can tell story after story. Or, you can spend less time on the factual details and give more "speaking time" to the stories. What you want your listeners to take away will be far more memorable. Trust me.

Should you open with a dramatic story, or end with one? Depends. If I open with a serious story, I make certain to bring in an equal measure of levity because I don't want to depress my audience. On the other hand, I often end with a dramatic note after a humorous talk because I think it shakes my audience up a bit. While they've had lots of fun listening to my message, I want them to know in the end that what I had to say was very important.

One example that comes to mind is my "Humor in the Workplace" speech. I'm very playful throughout that speech—all my stories are fun and upbeat—but I almost always end with this statement: "I want all of you to remember this: The average child laughs 200 times a day. The average adult, seven." I know that statistic really brings home the underlying message of my talk, and instantly they are slammed against the wall with that reality. That's good. It's exactly how I want to leave them; how I want to affect them.

Are there times to forego stories altogether? Not in the average speech or presentation. The recurring lesson in this book is to make certain you incorporate humor and good storytelling in all your speeches and presentations. The only possible exception might be if you're a participant on a panel, and your answers to the audience need to be short and sweet. Stories, in that instance, might be too long to share. But, again, in sum, I suggest that it would be a monumental mistake to do any future presentation or speech without a story or two.

Can a story go on too long? Yes, it can. One of the basic rules for storytelling is that each story be entertaining. If it goes on too long, it won't be. Make sure, then, that all your stories are "tight." In writer's parlance, that means you don't over-dialogue by going on and on. When you do (and I've seen speakers make this mistake), the audience gets restless and bored. So, for safety reasons, keep your stories quick and short, or make sure they have substantial build and intrigue to keep them entertaining and meaningful.

I'm going to expect that you won't venture forth from this point forward without the use of a good story in any speech or presentation that needs a good break here and there. (And, as I see it, that means virtually *every* speech and presentation.) Remember: Think balance! Take a stab at preparing stories by conceiving concepts for some, and then writing them out. Next, rehearse and rework them until they are tight and until they flow. This is a skill every speechmaker needs to master. In the end, it's what your audiences will remember you for.

And now, let's move on to the real deal, the "before" and "after" of a few speeches—a few versions without humor and good storytelling, and a few versions with them. I hope you'll notice a tremendous difference.

"... so, I say, 'Get over it Mortimer, it's only a cubicle. Throw it in the box with everything else and just take it with you...'"

Epilogue
Is *That* Funny?
Sample Speeches—
Before-and-After
Humor and Stories

It's time now to take a look at a few speeches, to consider the difference between the "dry" or "plain" approach—just the facts or basic information—and the "colorful" or "entertaining" way—the approach that's been the focus of this book! The point, of course, is to illustrate how the same material can come to life when humor and/or stories are added.

The first sample is a typical "intro." It's a mini-speech, if you will. It features a simple introduction of someone who is about to make a speech. We hear such speech "shorts" from panel moderators, speaker chairs, program directors and others who are ordinarily the first to take the lectern. Their job is to provide background information on the person or persons who are slated to fill the "speaking" portion of the event or gathering.

HOW DO YOU DO

Our intro speaker is Mr. Smith. Here goes:

MR. SMITH

Good evening, Ladies and Gentlemen, and welcome to the monthly meeting of the National Institute of Consumer Products. It is my pleasure to tell you that we have Joseph Miller with us tonight, who is going to talk to us about consumer trends. Joseph is currently on the board of IGS Products and MALFA. He has served as a volunteer for the Consumer Research Organization, and is currently writing a book on the most dramatic consumer trends of the 1900s and what we can expect during the first ten years of the new millennium. I've known Joseph for about a year now; I think we met last January…so without further adieu, let's welcome him…ladies and gentlemen…

As you can see, this is pretty standard in terms of an introduction. At the time of Smith's intro, chances are the people in the audience were just finishing dessert. (If I had been there I would have been starting to nap). Notice that Smith did nothing to capture their attention. I'll bet they weren't the least bit enticed into sitting up and listening—not only to Smith, but to poor Miller, who was about to take the lectern. So, for the sake of illustrating the heart and soul—the purpose—of this book, let's take another run at that introduction by Smith—that "show opener." Then, by comparing the two, I would like you to ask yourself which version is the one that would pique your interest.

This next take, of course, is what this book is all about—a speech that's dressed up with a bit of humor and a story.

MR. SMITH

Say, Ladies and Gentlemen…your attention please. **(He waits until the room has quieted down)** Tonight won't be just any night! Wait till you hear our speaker, Joseph Miller. **(Pregnant pause)** I guess the best way to introduce him is to tell you how I met him. Last January, after our regular Wednesday night meeting, I headed for the valet booth to get my car. I'm standing there—out front of the Marriott—and I hear this guy—or overhear this guy—talking to another guy. He's casually telling his friend, or business associate (I wasn't sure who he was talking to at the time), about his prediction of what types of technology were to be included as standard kitchen features in the home when the year 2015 rolls around. He's fascinating me with his comments. **(Laughs)** I'm trying not to let him know but I'm sort of following him—I couldn't tear myself away... So, as it turns out...I follow him all the way to his car...the valet was holding his car door open...(Thinking back, everyone else waiting for their cars probably thought I was some kind of carjacker or something)... Naturally, I realize I don't even know who this guy is, but I know I've just *got* to get him as a speaker at one our meetings! As he starts to get in his car, I introduce myself to him, shove my business card in his hand, and ask for his. When he sees I'm with the Institute, he seems impressed. Anyway, he must have been. When we had lunch the following week—he paid for it! And... Joseph Miller and I have been friends ever since. By the way, Joseph is on the board of IGS Products and MALFA. He's also been a volunteer for the Consumer Research Organization. He's writing a book on the most dramatic consumer trends that shaped our lives in the 1900s and what we can come to expect in the way of consumer trends in the first ten years of this new millennium. OOOOH, and just wait till you hear what some of them are going to be! Without further ado, ladies and gentlemen, I'd like to present to you Joseph Miller...**(Leads the audience in applause)**

As you can see, version #2 is far more enticing than version #1. It's also far more entertaining. Just like the savvy performer, in version #2 Smith waited for the audience to quiet down before he began, something many "intro" speakers never do. I know that, had I been in the audience for the second go-round, I certainly would have stopped to hear the story Smith shared. I would have saved my nap for after the meeting.

Notice first off how Smith's delivery in version #1 is rather "standard"—and downright bland, for that matter. Then check out the "connectable" approach the second time around. With regard to delivery, Smith is conversational—human and personable with his audience. In terms of his choice of content, he sets us up in an intriguing and enticing way. He also includes moments of humor and a fun little story about how he met the evening's speaker.

There is a vast difference between the two versions, and although I'm not suggesting that version #1 is the "wrong" way to provide an introduction, I am saying that it's pretty flat and boring. Version #2 (even though it takes a little more time) sets an entirely different tone. It creates a great sense of expectancy and anticipation for the audience. It is, in truth, far more entertaining. Ultimately, given the choice, it's the way in which each of us would prefer to hear that event's opening remarks.

You probably guessed it: Your next assignment is to write an "intro" for your next breakfast or dinner meeting. Try it a couple of different ways just for exercise. But one of your versions must include a bit of humor and a short anecdote or story.

Then, for fun, try each version out on a friend or business associate, and ask him or her which they would prefer hearing as a speaker introduction. Keep experimenting. Stay creative and most of all spontaneous. The key is to think "conversational." Have fun. Try to think of yourself in the audience and how you would react to your "intro." Once you've "worked out" this way, consider yourself a pro; it's what all the great stand-up comedians do—and the great storytellers—Jerry Seinfeld and Hal Holbrook among them.

In the end, your job is to entertain every audience, even if you're speaking for as little as one to five minutes. Put forth the effort to make sure that all your "intros" are attention-grabbers, in terms of both delivery and content.

Now let's move on to a couple of longer speeches—portions of them—and check out the before and after versions.

SPEAK NOW AND FOREVER HOLD US CAPTIVE

At first I thought it would be fun to dress up Lincoln's Gettysburg Address. But then I decided instead to offer a few typical speeches—the kind you or I might encounter in the workplace environment during the course of a seminar, training session, sales presentation, or group meeting. I've opted to work with parts of speeches—parts that would take only a few minutes—since the typical 45-minute or one-hour talk would eat up too much paper, and bore you as well, I'm sure!

The first speech I've chosen was given by a marketing expert whose intent was to inform his audience about the changes taking place in the advertising industry in view of the technology revolution. Let's skip the beginning remarks and get right into the heart of his message:

SPURLOCK

...so as I was saying, the advertising industry will probably change more drastically than any other one in the coming years. Most every sales message will be done electronically—either through video or the Internet. Technology is simply taking over. The capability brochure, as we know it, may soon be extinct. You may only see such explanatory material on a Web site. I know at our agency, we discourage our clients from printing too many materials because in this "experience economy," everyone wants to be entertained. That seemingly comes only through some type of technology. I know I certainly like to be sold through the latest fast paced visual advances. So then, what can we expect in this new millennium? Presentations, ad campaigns, sales and promotional tools that tend to entertain us. I think the corporate world is becoming spoiled. When someone is trying to sell the business professional in the business sector today, they expect a show. If there's not some pizzazz or drama to accompany the message, then people may not be motivated to buy. I think we all need to get more creative—and I don't mean bizarre, just inventive—in order to stand out from the competition. If your ad campaign from last year didn't do the job, then ask your marketing team what you can do this year to get the job done...

All right. Spurlock is making a point, and a very important one. He's doing an okay job. Notice, though, how he's just spewing ideas and opinions at his audience without underscoring them with meaningful or illustrative examples—examples that could have been beautifully provided through good stories and humor. Remember what I've said all along: We need to stay with the "who" and the "why"—bring things back to the human level—to drive our points home. The "what"—the facts and basics—can be more secondary).

Though I felt Spurlock was dead on—his points were valid ones—I wasn't moved or inspired by his talk because his content seemed to lack human interest. Also, he didn't endear me to himself. I didn't laugh. I wasn't touched in any profound, satiric or ironic way, either, because there was neither humor nor storytelling. I found it hard to relate. Once again: Don't forget why the typical well-skilled stand-up comic is so successful. While he's making his points, he is doing so in a way that brings the points home to each of us. He does this via two things: stories and humor.

With that in mind, let's take Spurlock's speech segment for a second spin and add a little humor and storytelling; making it more alive as well as interesting and entertaining. By the way, I found it ironic that the very person who was trying to convince us that we needed to be more exciting and entertaining in putting forth our sales messages wasn't doing much himself in that regard to sell his points! At any rate, here we go:

SPURLOCK

(**Smiling**)...so as I was saying, the advertising industry will probably change more drastically than any other in the coming years. (**Chuckling**) And God help the technically impaired! Most every sales message will be done electronically—especially through the Internet. The Net is like Godzilla—it's storming the marketplace and stepping all over conventional advertising means. (**Pause**) And how about the

Net's television ads. Wow, those are some of the most clever deliveries I've *ever* seen. They are always *so* funny! **(Shakes his head slightly. Then stops to ponder)** How about the chimp who was flanked by two old fogies in that ad on Superbowl Sunday? You probably saw it. Remember? The chimp was wildly **(Imitates the chimp with slightly flailing arms)** conducting some out-of-view orchestra. **(Beat. Then a frown)** "What the heck is it doing?", I asked myself. **(Beat. Intense. Fists clutching air)** That ad grabbed you and held you. You had no idea what they were selling. Then, of course, at the end, a simple headline popped up over that **(Smiling)** hilarious visual: **(Changes voice to sound like an announcer)** "We've just wasted two million bucks. What are you doing with your money?" And suddenly you saw the E*trade name and logo. **(Shakes head again)** Gee, I wish I could get a copy of that. **(Beat. Almost under his breath, ruefully)** I'd like to see it right after every one of my golf games just to cheer myself up. **(Emphatic)** That's my point: You can't help but smile and have good feelings when you recall that commercial image. **(Beat)** Well, that's where we're going. **(Laughingly)** Advertisers are out to thoroughly entertain us with a one-two punch. No more ads like the Playtex bra one that showed us *how* the product works. **(Grimaces)** Would that even be politically correct today? **(Casually)** Anyway, we just need a hard-hitting sound bite to get us off our duffs. **(Looks into space and thinks a moment)** Now...if the chimp was doing that ad for Playtex...well...never mind.... And hey, how about the capability brochure! Those will be like exotic wildlife! Few and far between, I'm afraid. **(Slight chuckle)** Try to find one in ten years. It wouldn't surprise me if someday the Smithsonian had an entire *building* dedicated to the brochure, showing off the best of... **(Groping for the right words and picturing it in his mind)** I can see it now, people gawking, taking pictures—some exuberant brochure-collector yelling: **(Changes voice to sound like a loud-mouthed Midwesterner)** "Hey, Ethel, quick. Come here, look at this gloss-coated IBM cover. Oooh, aaaah, I bet that was a four-color job...and hot doggie, look at the stock it's on!" **(Laughs with the audience. Beat)** My point is this: everyone wants to take part in the "experience economy." So entertainment is the byword. That's what we can expect in this new millennium. More E*trade-type ads—creativity—and much of it humorous... **(Serious)** all of which will be slanted in that genre. **(Pause)** So when you're thinking about presentations, ad campaigns—sales *and* promotional tools—**(Passionate)** think clever—think exciting—think "E"—think about how *you* can use technology to scoop your competition. **(Pause)** See, everyone is intrigued by the new and the unexpected. **(Teasingly)** The word "show" has a double meaning, my friends! **(Direct)** If there's not some pizzazz or drama to accompany the message, then people may not be motivated to buy what it is you're selling. **(Big finish)** Get creative—not bizarre—just inventive. Remember: You want to stand out *from* the competition. **(Reconsidering for a moment...)** Close your eyes for a minute. Think about your ad campaign from last year. Did it do the job? Now, picture it. **(Long pause)** Okay, open your eyes now. **(Enthusiastically pointing out toward the audience)** All right—who has a campaign from last year they can tell us about and...oh, good **(Finger stops. Pointing now to one of the persons with a raised hand)** and after you tell us about this campaign, **(Knowingly)** how about spontaneously sharing how the use of technology could have *enhanced* it...

As you can see, this version is more hard-hitting. It offers a few "punchlines;" a couple of analogies; some examples; and finishes by inviting the audience to take part in a quick aside. I don't know about you, but I would much prefer version #2 because it makes me feel attached to the speaker; it entertains me and most certainly makes the points far more vivid. Now, you might be saying, "Yes, but it's longer." True, but my theory is you can cut other places that are simply over-explanations or superfluous. In other words, you can substitute some of the "entertaining" material for stuff that is boring or redundant and end up with a speech or presentation that is exactly the same in length and time. Truth be told, many speeches have dispensable content. So I'm suggesting that you pick and choose carefully. Save the expositional for the entertaining segments. Cut back on the dry parts. Keep them short and to the point. Then you'll always have enough time for the entertaining portions. I believe that most audiences have no sense of time when they're entertained. But they certainly begin to watch the clock when a speech is sluggish, predictable, or downright boring.

Naturally, you know what's next: I'd like you to take just a small portion of any speech or presentation you have given or are about to give and revamp the segment—adding a dash of humor and perhaps a story or two. An invitation for an interactive segment with the audience is something else I want you to consider adding. Then take your "before" and "after" versions and try them out on someone you trust. See what their preference is? Also, tape yourself and take a look. Which makes *you* want to be in your audience?

AS DRY AS A DRONE

I offer the next two speech segment examples to reinforce what I've been teaching throughout this book. The two are vastly different from the above, and I hope they convince you that *any* speech segment has the potential for humor and/or storytelling.

The first one is as dry as a speech can be! It happens to be a passage from a message given to the board of directors of Qlogic, a very successful computer-support company in southern California. The CEO of that company, H.K. Desai, is a client and a friend of mine. Though this is what the chairman of the board asked of him, I found it unfortunate, because Mr. Desai has a fabulous sense of humor; he's one of the most spontaneous and lovable speakers I've had the pleasure of coaching. He also has a natural charisma that just got buried during this "performance." I would have given anything if he had been given the chance to be himself and add just a smidgen of his own magic. In our second take, I'll offer up just a taste of what I think he could have added—even though this was intended to be a very serious and straight-ahead piece of dialogue.

DESAI

...another key trend driving the growth of the I/O market today is the increased number and variety of peripheral devices that are routinely attached to computers. In addition to a core hard drive, computers are increasingly equipped with accessory peripherals, such as tape drives for backup and archival, CD-Roms for multi-media and program installation, and removable hard-disk drives that offer a high-capacity alternative to floppy-disk drives. High-end workstations and servers often connect to high-performance storage arrays known as raid systems. These new peripherals have created incremental revenue opportunities for Qlogic.

Ho-hum! In terms of verbiage, this is pretty plain. It's technical and very dry. And that's why I chose this example: I wanted to show you how you could take even the most basic technical dialogue and dress it up.

Here we go with "Take Two":

DESAI

...another key trend driving the growth of the I/O market today is the increased number and variety of peripheral devices that are routinely attached to computers. If that's eye-opening, just think what it'll be like a few years from now, when virtually everything we use in our daily lives will be attached to a computer...**(Pause)** hey, toast at the click of a mouse might not be too far-fetched... gee, in that case, pretty soon it might take only ten minutes to whip up an entire Thanksgiving dinner...**(Laughs)** ...at any rate, in addition to a core hard drive, computers are increasingly equipped with accessory peripherals such as tape drives for backup and archival, CD-Roms for multi-media and program installation, and removable hard-disk drives that offer a high-capacity alternative to floppy-disk drives. **(Pause. Pensive)** You know, I find this amazing because, when I first started in this industry as an engineer—and it wasn't all that long ago, either—we only dreamed of these possibilities! I remember sitting with a few colleagues late one night, drinking our umpteenth cup of coffee, when someone in the room longingly asked: "Do you think one day we'll ever have alternatives to floppy disk drives?" We almost pelted him with styrofoam cups. Heck, we were thrilled to have any kind of disks at all at that time. Boy, have we come a long way! Now, high-end work stations and servers often connect to high-performance storage arrays know as raid systems. So these new peripherals have created incremental **(A little smug)** and, I might add, pretty attractive revenue opportunities for Qlogic. **(Smiling)** You know the old adage about opportunity knocking...well, I'd just like to say: Opportunities are *banging* down our door and we're ready to welcome each and every one of them!

I'm not suggesting that this is the way Mr. Desai should have delivered this passage. In his situation, he may have felt more comfortable just dishing out the facts—and nothing but the facts. I do believe, however, had I been one of the board members, I would have been listening far more intently to the way the information was imparted in the second version. I also would have sensed confidence and pride from Mr. Desai, ultimately leaving me with a "feel-good" mindset at the conclusion of his remarks. Even the most "Wall Street" types appreciate a little humor and verve!

TRAINING WHEELS

This last example is a speech given by Steve Kight, a very energetic and dynamic speaker—an executive for Nissan (Infiniti)—who was also short-changed because he was somewhat restricted in what he could say. His speech was on a TelePrompTer and he had to follow it word-for-word. I just know that had he been able to deviate just a bit, or been allowed to write his own speech, it would have been very different.

Again, I am covering only a small portion of his talk. His portion of this presentation took place at a dealer meeting before the company's franchise owners:

KIGHT

...As you remember, the original launch training program required you to send your staff to Scottsdale for a week...which, of course, is not practical today.

Instead, we will put the training on the road with a ten-city tour. This training will be for all dealership employees. In addition, we will have specific job-skills training for service staff and management, as well as for parts and parts management...

Once again, pretty dry stuff. I'd like to take a second pass at this short segment and give it the humor and storytelling treatment, just to illustrate how—given the option—this information can be imparted in a far more entertaining way.

KIGHT

...As you remember, the original launch training program required you to send your staff to Scottsdale for a week...**(Pause. A little self-pity)** Gee, I don't remember anybody asking me to go along. But, that's okay because today, of course, it's not practical. **(A second thought)** In fact, it's never practical to go to Scottsdale, is it? **(Inquisitive)** ...Ever pay a greens fee in that town? Ha! I could buy a whole house for one day at Gray Hawk!

So, instead of Scottsdale, it looks like we will put the training on the road with a ten-city tour. This training will be for all dealership employees. In addition, we will have specific job-skills training for service staff and management as well as for parts and parts management. **(Beat)** Wonder if that training includes a golf lesson? Don't laugh. I remember when I first started with Nissan and I was going through a two-week training program. Someone kiddingly told me part of the training would include a golf lesson and I kept waiting...**(Beat)** truth is, **(Beat)** I'm still waiting!

As you can see, there is a very different tone with the addition of a few "asides." You catch a glimpse of Mr. Kight's personality and walk away with a very different feeling about him as a presenter. Some may argue that the changes in the last two scripts might not be appropriate, and that could be true; content and delivery choices do depend upon circumstances and the audience. I'm simply trying to point out possibilities to stimulate your imagination for those speech segments that *could* be punched up and enlivened with humor or stories.

In the end, where and when to insert humor and stories will be up to you. I used these examples so you could realize that any speech—any portion of a speech—can include either (or both) humor and good stories to enrich them.

WRITE AWAY

What might prove a fun and challenging assignment would be to take all three of the above speech segments and rewrite second versions that would reflect your own ideas in the way of humor and stories. It would certainly be a terrific way to put all your new-found knowledge to work. I urge you to try it!

But even if you opt not to do that homework, your challenge now—and from here on out—is to find places where you can inject a little humor or a great story. I tell all my students to take each speech or presentation and separate it into chunks, providing each chunk with a hearty helping of humor and stories. You can always decide to delete one, or, add another—or, too, chose places where it might be fun just to improvise. **The goal is to put together material that would entertain you if you were an audience member.** The goal is also to perfect your delivery, so that when you do present such great material, your performance is that of a total professional.

One last note: As you go about your work, do so only with *reasonable* caution (i.e, political correctness, good taste, etc.). I don't want you to limit or restrict yourself unnecessarily, because, quite frankly, that's probably what you've been doing all along. Instead, I want you to swing free and dig deep into your bountiful resources. Use all your humor. Tell all your stories. I know they are there for you to use, share, and enjoy!

My wish for you is that the next time someone says, "What's so funny?" everyone instantly turns and nods at you!

ABOUT THE AUTHOR

A founding member of the world-famous L.A. Groundlings, Cherie Kerr is the founder, and since 1990, the Executive Producer and Artistic Director of the Orange County Crazies, a sketch and improvisational comedy troupe in Santa Ana, California. She also serves as the group's head writer. She has received rave reviews for her work both as a writer and director.

Kerr has taught improvisational comedy to actors for the past 30 years, and teaches other classes as well, including a class on how to develop original characters and how to write sketch comedy. She has studied with some of the best improv and comedy teachers in the business, including Gary Austin, founder of the L.A. Groundlings, and a former member of the highly acclaimed group, The Committee; Michael Gellman, a director and teacher for Second City, in Chicago; and Jeannie Berlin (an Academy Award nominee and Elaine May's daughter). In her formative years, she studied at the Pasadena Academy of Drama.

Kerr founded ExecuProv in 1983, and has provided a variety of classes on presentation and communication skills to hundreds of business professionals. Her clients include ARCO, Nissan Motors, Mitsubishi, Ingram Micro, Bank One, Delta Dental, Foothill Capital, PacifiCare, Universal Studios, Condor Freight Lines, Boise Cascade, Office Depot and the U.S. Naval Academy at Annapolis. She also has worked for a number of governmental agencies including the L.A. City Attorney's Office, the L.A. District Attorney's Office, and the County of Orange. She is a certified Provider for the Continuing Legal Education Program for the State Bar of California, and has served as that organization's official speaker-trainer for its Board of Governors.

A writer for more than 30 years, Kerr has owned an award-winning public relations firm and still works as an occasional consultant in that field. She has written, produced and directed an original full-scale musical comedy, is a member of ASCAP, and has been honored as an award-winning journalist and publicist. Kerr was named, along with Disney's Michael Eisner, as one of the "Top Ten Most Sensational People in Orange County," by *Orange Coast Magazine*. She is also a humor columnist and has been written about in a number of publications including the *Harvard Review Communication Newsletter*.

Kerr also starred in her own one-woman show, *Out Of Her Mind*, which was met with great success and which she single-handedly wrote. In it she played a number of original characters. She also played Barbara Walters, much to the audience's delight.

In addition to lecturing and teaching ExecuProv, both in classroom situations and in private, one-on-one tutoring sessions, Kerr provides speechwriting services for many of her clients. Kerr also provides her creative services to large companies for corporate comedy industrials.

Kerr is frequently sought out as a keynote speaker addressing presentation and communication skills and humor in the workplace.

In addition to *"What's So Funny?"*, Kerr has written a book on one-on-one communication in the workplace, *"When I Say This...," "Do You Mean That?"*, as well as a book on public speaking skills, *"I've Asked Miller To Say A Few Words,"* both of which use improv comedy techniques as the basis for the lessons. She also has written a book on sketch comedy: *Build to Laugh: How to Construct Sketch Comedy With the Fast and Funny Formula*, a sketch writing book. Currently in the works is *How To Think Fast On Your Feet (Without Putting Them In Your Mouth)*, a manual to help business professionals handle pressure and tension during difficult communication situations.

In addition to her self-help books, Kerr is also authoring a novel about her father's life as a jazz string-bassist, *Charlie's Notes*.

She resides in Santa Ana, California. The mother of three also has three grandchildren.